IS JESUS
WORTH IT?

Stacey thacker

HARVEST HOUSE PUBLISHERS
EUGENE, OREGON

Unless otherwise indicated, all Scripture quotations are from The ESV® Bible (The Holy Bible, English Standard Version®), copyright © 2001 by Crossway, a publishing ministry of Good News Publishers. Used by permission. All rights reserved.

Verses marked The Voice are taken from The Voice™. Copyright © 2008 by Ecclesia Bible Society. Used by permission. All rights reserved.

Verses marked MSG are taken from THE MESSAGE. Copyright © by Eugene H. Peterson 1993, 1994, 1995, 1996, 2000, 2001, 2002. Used by permission of Tyndale House Publishers, Inc.

Verses marked PHILLIPS are taken from J.B. Phillips: The New Testament in Modern English, Revised Edition. © J.B. Phillips 1958, 1960, 1972. Used by permission of Macmillan Publishing Company.

Verses marked NASB are taken from the New American Standard Bible®, © 1960, 1962, 1963, 1968, 1971, 1972, 1973, 1975, 1977, 1995 by The Lockman Foundation. Used by permission. (www.Lockman.org)

Verses marked NIV are taken from the Holy Bible, New International Version®, NIV®. Copyright © 1973, 1978, 1984, 2011 by Biblica, Inc.® Used by permission. All rights reserved worldwide.

Verses marked KJV are taken from the King James Version of the Bible.

Cover by Connie Gabbert Design + Illustration

Interior design by Janelle Coury

Cover images © Mila Petkova / Shutterstock; Stephen Rees / Shutterstock

Published in association with Books & Such Management, 52 Mission Circle, Suite 122, PMB 170, Santa Rosa, CA 95409-5370, www.booksandsuch.com.

IS JESUS WORTH IT?

Copyright © 2017 Stacey Thacker
Published by Harvest House Publishers
Eugene, Oregon 97402
www.harvesthousepublishers.com

ISBN 978-0-7369-7008-2 (pbk.)
ISBN 978-0-7369-7009-9 (eBook)

All rights reserved. No part of this publication may be reproduced, stored in a retrieval system, or transmitted in any form or by any means—electronic, mechanical, digital, photocopy, recording, or any other—except for brief quotations in printed reviews, without the prior permission of the publisher.

Printed in the United States of America

17 18 19 20 21 22 23 24 25 / BP-JC / 10 9 8 7 6 5 4 3 2 1

For Mom
Thank you for loving and
living God's Word every day of your life.

Acknowledgments

Mike: Thank you for your never-ending support and seeing the writer in me first. Love you. Always.

Emma, Abby, Caroline, and Alison: You are the best girls in the world. I know it to be true. Thank you for letting me get all excited about writing and not complaining too much when I go to Panera to work. I love you so much!

Lisa Chudy: Thank you for signing me up for Hebrews, not asking my permission, and mostly for saving me a seat next to you.

Robin Langford: I will always credit our friendship to God's Word. I can't think of anyone better to do *life* with than you. Thanks for everything.

Tanya Cramer: I am so very grateful for your work behind the scenes on every word written in this book. You are a rare gift, my friend. I treasure you!

Emily Blackwell, Erin Warren, Teri Lynne Underwood, and Angie Elkins: You have read words and listened to me talk endlessly about this project. What would I do without you?

Kathleen Kerr: Some people are scared of their editors. I want to buy you all the coffee and tell you wholeheartedly that I am truly blessed. Your gifts make my work so much easier.

Harvest House Team: I am tremendously blessed to be part of what God is doing at Harvest House. Thank you for being more like family than publishers.

Janet Grant: Thank you for seeing the "Girlfriend" in the "Guide" and just knowing how to make this work. You are the best!

Jesus: You are worth it.

CONTENTS

Introduction

Have you ever started something and then wondered what in the world you were thinking? I'm reminded of the scene in the movie *Tangled* when Rapunzel bravely steps out of her comfortable tower room, where she's been sheltered most of her life. As she takes her leap of faith into the unknown, she joyously exclaims, "Best day ever!" However, in the next scene she is a weepy hot mess, lamenting her decision and branding herself a failure. She tumbles from heights of happiness to depths of despair, back and forth, over and over again.

This is a book based on a book of the Bible. Writing it has me experiencing all the feelings a girl can feel. I have bravely stepped out of my own comfortable tower room into what feels like the unknown.

On one hand, I'm ridiculously excited because I love the idea of inspiring you to put down this book and pick up the Book that truly matters. I've said it before, and it bears repeating: The one book I want you to read more than mine is the Bible. My passion for God's Word has only grown as I've placed myself at his feet and said time and time again, "What do you want your daughters to know about your book, Lord?" He has been faithful. I have been moved to tears more than once by his nearness and direction.

At other times, I find myself facedown on my bed, questioning my calling. I wonder what in the world I'm doing trying to pen words about holy things. I have quit so many times in my head. I've assured

myself my editor would be grateful if I just sent the contract back and
said, "Truly, you have the wrong girl." Surely they would receive my
regrets with relief. Surely.

Have you ever felt that way about something you were sure God
wanted you to do? Did doubts creep in and give sway? What did you
do about it? Did you pray? Phone a friend? Post on Facebook? Maybe,
like me, you did all three. I like to have all my bases covered, you know.

Teri Lynne is the girlfriend I knew I needed in my own best day-
worst day moment last week. She told me it was okay to second-guess
myself as long as I remembered who this work was truly about. She
even loaned me a prayer: "Don't ever let me think, dear God, that I was
anything but the instrument for your story."[1]

The author of these words, Flannery O'Conner, struggled with this
back and forth in her head as well. She was in college when she wrote
that simple prayer. I was so moved by it I wrote it on the memo board
in my kitchen and prayed it back to God while I was making dinner
that night. It is such a sweet and timely reminder. The important thing
for each of us to remember is that this is God's story, not ours. As we
place ourselves in his hands, he fills the pages of our lives with holy
words that overflow into the lives of others if we let them.

I think maybe I get so worried because I care about God's Word
tremendously. I have a passion for other women to find the sweet treasure of his truth for themselves. I believe with all my heart if you and
I are going to endure to the end, we are going to need God's Word to
get us through the tough days. That Word is absolutely vital to our
being able to say, "Jesus is worth it," because Jesus is the Word made
flesh (John 1:14).

The Word made flesh is worth it.

Even with Teri Lynne's encouragement and Flannery's prayer, I was
still wavering back and forth between my own "Best day ever!" and
"What have I done?" As I ping-ponged back and forth, I began to think
about when I first fell in love with God's Word.

In college, I would spend hours poring over the Word of God in
part because I had the time. It seemed whenever I opened the Bible I

found a new truth to apply. Years later, after marriage and motherhood and life settled in with more time constraints and hardship aplenty, I stumbled into the book of Hebrews a bit jaded. But the sweetness of God's Word wooed my heart and extended an invitation to the mercy I desperately needed.

How about you? When did you fall in love with the Word of God? Was it when you read a particular Bible story? During a certain time in your life? When you learned to study the Bible on your own? Did a skilled teacher help you find the Word a joy? Did switching to a different translation make the difference?

I can relate to each of these because God has done the same for me. My friend Candace beautifully shared her own story with me, and it brought tears to my eyes.

> During a very dark and difficult season in my life, God drew me in with his love letter. I grew up doing Bible studies and loved that aspect of studying God's Word, but this was different. God was wooing me and comforting me in ways I hadn't experienced before. A deeper love for God's Word grew out of that dark season. He truly was my only light. He spoke to me so clearly through the pages of his Word, and I learned more of our faithful God through those sweet moments with him.

His Word is not only a love letter but a life-changing tool in our hands.

I've lived this. God drew Candace into his Word to comfort and encourage her during dark and difficult times. His Word is not only a love letter but a life-changing tool in our hands. It leads us to mercy. And oh, girls, we are going to need all the mercy for the days that lie ahead.

Who am I kidding? We need all the mercy right now.

A Girlfriend's Guide to the Bible (a Series)

Whenever I write I have a couple of things in mind. First, my passion is to point you to Jesus and his life-giving Word. My prayer is that when you put down one of my books, you will want to know God better. The book I want you to really dive into is his, not mine. When I look back over my life, every time I found myself in a deep, deep pit, the one thing that made it possible for me to climb out was the Word of God. I take great comfort in the promise of Isaiah 40:8: "The grass withers, the flower fades, but the word of our God will stand forever." God's Word will not wither even when I think I might. And when my heart would rather fade into the background, God is just getting started. His Word is perpetual, unending, and continuous. So is the healing he wants to bring into my life and yours. Life lived with and for Jesus really does just keep getting better.

Second, I want you to feel as though you know me. I want you to see I'm just like you. I prefer a drive-thru, I drink way too much coffee, and I enjoy singing loudly and embarrassing my daughters. My hope is that we can connect on the normal things in life, as girlfriends do. We may not have met in real life yet, but we are more alike than you know.

As I prayed about the next books I would write, God began to unfold the idea of a series just for girlfriends like us. It would be a set of books, based on books of the Bible, that sound more like a conversation over coffee than a sermon. We would laugh and cry together (obviously), but in the end we would truly fall deeper in love with Jesus.

I should probably put a small disclaimer here. I am not a theologian or even a seminary graduate. I'm simply a girl who has a passion for studying God's Word and I've been doing it for almost 30 years. This series is not a commentary of the Bible. It is not comprehensive. I couldn't possibly cover every detail in every book of the Bible. What you will find are books *inspired* by books of the Bible. I will purposely leave a few things out and I promise you I will jump around a bit. Hey, that's what girlfriends do, right? We'll always have more to talk about the next time we meet. For example, you might want to know the next book in this series will be based on Ephesians (you can read more about that in my note at the end of this book). I'm already praying about it even now as I'm introducing you to Hebrews.

Book 1—Hebrews: Is Jesus Worth It?

If you asked me what my favorite book of the Bible is, I would say Hebrews without hesitation. It has been my "pit" book. The one that lifted me from the depths of despair and has given me the strength I needed to put one foot in front of the other. It also has a great deal of Old Testament within its pages, which makes writing through it a dream. And Hebrews is one of the most Jesus-focused books in the Bible. Next to the four Gospels, Hebrews has more direct references to Christ than any other book.

Have you ever wanted to quit your faith journey? The Hebrews did. In your heart, have you ever wondered, "Is Jesus worth it?" The Hebrews did. In fact, they almost turned back to the life they had before they met Christ. They were a group of primarily Jewish believers who'd been raised with the Old Testament Law as their guidepost. Rules ruled, you might say. At the time the letter of Hebrews was written, they were facing a few trials and knew that more would come. Going back to what felt comfortable just seemed to make sense to them. Or maybe they could simply put their own spin on their new-found Christian faith. Surely no one would notice if they did that.

I am tempted to do this myself. Maybe I can be all Jesus wants me to be but hold back some of my own hopes and dreams for myself. I mean, when I sing "I Surrender All" perhaps I don't have to mean it 100 percent. Can I surrender 98.9 percent instead? God would be okay with that, wouldn't he? Or perhaps it's okay to need God and the approval of everyone around me at the same time? It's good to be "liked" and accepted, right?

When life gets particularly hard, I know these are the thoughts running through my head and my heart too. Sound familiar?

Sweet friend, trials will come. Your faith will be tested. God wants you to know your faith can endure and be ignited when it finds its true source of life in Jesus. He is the heart, the help, and the hope we need when trials come our way.

Together, we are going to take a long look at Jesus. We're going to unveil our own hearts and see what idols may be fighting for our attention. We're going to fix our eyes on the author and perfecter of our faith. We're going to dive deep into the pages of his Word. Mostly, we will be in Hebrews, but we will also visit other books of the Bible. Everything in the Word truly is connected. But most importantly, we're going to answer the question, "Is Jesus worth it?" together, because that is what girlfriends do.

I can't wait to get started.

Looking forward,

Stacey

How to Use This Book

Please do me a favor. Read this book with your own Bible nearby. Maybe you have a beat up 20-year-old Bible like I do. Or maybe you recently purchased a journaling Bible. I love those! Or perhaps you use your smartphone or computer when you study God's Word. Whatever works for you, have it with you as you read. I want you to be able to find the verses we talk about and mark them so you can easily find them later. Just remember to keep the "guide" in "Girlfriend's Guide" in mind. My greatest prayer is that when you're finished reading *Is Jesus Worth It?* you won't be able to wait to investigate on your own.

At the beginning of each chapter you'll find a list of some key Scripture references. You might want to start by reading through them to prepare your heart for the words that follow.

You can of course read this book on your own and journal your way through it. I love doing that. But I've also put together a group study guide at the end of the book. My hope is that you'll invite a few girlfriends to walk through the book with you and let the guide do the work for you. Just read the chapters, all show up at your favorite coffee place, and answer the questions. And remember, I'm praying for you!

PART 1

The Heart, Hope, and
Help We Have in Jesus

1

Start with Worship

I have nothing to preach but Jesus.

CHARLES SPURGEON

Hebrews 1:1-3; Matthew 9:20-22; Isaiah 6:1-8

We don't even know her name. She might have been 25 or 40. Was she married or single? She could have been a sister or a mother. Maybe she was a lot like you and me. What we do know is her life was one of pain and suffering of the cruelest kind. She was a broken-down woman desperate for change.

I think this woman living by the shores of Capernaum must have been following Jesus from a safe distance for quite some time—listening, seeking, and hoping he could help her. Up until now, no one else had been able to. Would he? Could he?

Scripture gives us the tiniest glimpse of the moment before the moment she reached out. I suspect she was having a full-blown conversation inside her own heart. Did she count the cost? Did she have doubts? She must have, "for she said to herself, 'If I only touch his garment, I will be made well'" (Matthew 9:21). This unnamed, faceless woman was having a crisis of faith, but she must have believed the risk was worth it for she extended her hand to brush the tasseled hem of his robe. *Jesus was worth it.* He had fueled her faith precisely at the moment she felt like quitting. And so with faith as small as a mustard seed, she reached for him.

This was all it took, and what happened next is one of my favorite encounters in the Bible. "Jesus turned, and seeing her he said, 'Take heart, daughter; your faith has made you well.' And instantly the woman was made well" (Matthew 9:22).

> The millions of moments she had collected before this one no longer mattered. She was no longer *woman unclean*. She was *daughter made well*.

Jesus saw her and uttered the words she dreamed of hearing. "Made well" he said. He spoke courage to a girl who had known nothing but a daily reminder that she was broken. Did you notice he called her not *woman*, but *daughter*? We can hear so much tenderness in this one sentence. Women in her condition were not called *daughter*. They were called *unclean*. But Jesus erased that label with a word. Her faith, an act of worship, made her well in an instant. The millions of moments she had collected before this one no longer mattered. She was no longer *woman unclean*. She was *daughter made well*.

I don't know about you, but I want the kind of faith that passes through the crisis point and reaches out anyway. I want to hear him say to me, "Take heart, daughter; your faith has made you well." Are you asking yourself if Jesus is worth it? Do you feel like quitting? Are your heart and head in complete disagreement over whether you should reach out to brush the hem of Jesus's garment? We don't have much to bring to the table besides our messy lives and minuscule faith. Our inner conversations don't scare Jesus away either, because they don't change who he is. He stands ready to fuel our faith in the most amazing way, if only we will take a look and extend our hand.

Sweet friends, this is our moment before the moment. Let's take a deep breath and reach out—together.

My Own Crisis of Faith

Years ago I was a broken-down desperate woman too. I didn't have much left in me at the time. To be honest, I was in a pretty scary place. I had been following Jesus at a distance, waiting and wondering if he was aware of my pain and, honestly, if he cared. I knew one thing for sure: either my situation needed to change or I did.

I had the feeling the pit I'd plunged into headlong was not quite finished swallowing me whole. You see, my husband and I had felt the stirring from the Lord to surrender our lives and follow him into full-time ministry. We were certain of it. But the circumstances during this time screamed otherwise. It was almost as if when we said a resounding yes to God, we also said yes to a whole mess of trials. Those tribulations seemed dead set on scaring us into running the complete opposite direction. Don't think for a minute I didn't consider it. I thought, *If this is how Jesus treats his friends, I can't imagine how he treats his enemies.* I was worn thin by it all.

> Instead of hitting rock bottom I ran right into Jesus—arms-open-wide, beautiful, truth-telling Jesus.

With this all going on in the background, my friend Lisa signed me up for Bible study. She didn't ask me if I wanted to go with her. She just casually added at the end of one of our phone conversations, "Hey, Stacey, I signed you up for a Bible study on the book of Hebrews. You can sit by me. Oh, and there's free child care." Without waiting for my answer, she hung up. She was wonderfully sneaky like that.

I showed up on a Thursday at midday, with my two-year-old in tow, my beat-up study Bible, and a plate of cookies. I sat down next to Lisa and exhaled. The leader opened her notes and started sharing from the first chapter of Hebrews, and I was forever changed. Instead of hitting rock bottom I ran right into Jesus—arms-open-wide, beautiful, truth-telling Jesus. As it turned out, he did care. I touched his hem for the first time in ages, forgot about why, and worshiped.

Start with Jesus

The writer of Hebrews starts bold and just keeps moving. He has a go-big-or-go-home attitude I find inspiring. He starts by preaching Jesus and nothing else.

> Long ago, at many times and in many ways, God spoke to our fathers by the prophets, but in these last days he has spoken to us by his Son, whom he appointed the heir of all things, through whom also he created the world. He is the radiance of the glory of God and the exact imprint of his nature, and he upholds the universe by the word of his power. After making purification for sins, he sat down at the right hand of the Majesty on high (1:1-3).

The fact that the writer doesn't identify himself has led to a debate about who penned this valuable letter. Some believe it to be Paul. The 1611 version of the King James Bible listed Paul as the writer. Others have argued that Barnabas had the authority to write it. Still, many believe the writer to be Apollos, as suggested by Martin Luther.

We will most likely never know who wrote the letter of Hebrews, but we do know a few things about him. He was a Greek-speaking, well-educated Jew who converted to Christianity. He had a strong knowledge of the Greek Old Testament called the Septuagint. We also have strong evidence that the writer was a second-generation believer who might have come to faith through the ministry of the apostles.

The writer isn't going to bother telling us important stuff we usually include in letters, like who he is, to whom he is writing, or even why he is writing. With a laser focus and a quill, he cuts to the heart of the matter. He starts with Jesus because he knows this is what his readers truly needed. "For, after all," Charles Spurgeon wrote, "this is the subject which men most of all need. They may have cravings after other things, but nothing can satisfy the deep real want of their nature but Jesus Christ and salvation by his precious blood. He is the Bread of life which came down from heaven; he is the Water of life whereof, if a man drink, he shall never thirst again."[1]

> Our deep, real want finds a deep well
> of satisfaction only in Christ.

The writer of Hebrews knew everything else grows dim when we first fix our eyes on Jesus. He knew, long before Charles Spurgeon said it, that our deep, real want finds a deep well of satisfaction only in Christ. We may chase after other things, but they will never truly satisfy us.

Think for a minute about the last thing you thought you wanted. Was it a day at the spa, a new cardigan, or a date with a special someone? When you got it, did it bring you satisfaction of a lasting kind? Was that satisfaction sustainable over days and weeks? Or did it fade—and did you find your heart longing for something to replace it? Girls, our hearts were meant for more. Our hearts were meant to worship Jesus. Why would we start anywhere else?

When I sat in that Bible study so long ago, my deep, real want was security. I wanted everything in my life to be safe. Fear was waging a war in my heart. One look at Jesus in Hebrews chapter 1, and my deep, real want saw something I could plant my faith in. I saw that *Jesus* was the final word, the fullness of God's glory, faithful to hold all things together, and he finished the work of salvation.

The Final Word

God's nature is to speak. He has spoken from the beginning and in many ways.

- God spoke creation into being from nothingness (Genesis 1).
- God spoke directly to Moses, face-to-face (Numbers 12:8).
- God spoke to his people through the prophets of old who had dreams and saw visions (Joel 2:28).

John Piper brings all this into perspective for us.

> God is not withdrawn and uncommunicative...He was not

silent. God communicates. He means to connect with us. He is not an idea to be thought about. He is a person to be listened to and understood and enjoyed and obeyed. He is a speaking Person. There is no more important fact than this: There is a God who speaks that we might know him and love him and live in joyful obedience to him. God spoke.[2]

Our creative God is a communicator. He is a speaking person who wants us to know him and love him. The thread of his speaking voice is strong throughout all of Scripture. But according to the writer of Hebrews, in these last days God did something different. He ceased speaking in many ways and spoke to us by his Son. His Son was his final Word. And his final Word was better than all former communication. Why? The book of John gives us a tiny glimpse.

In the beginning was the Word, and the Word was with God, and the Word was God. He was in the beginning with God. All things were made through him, and without him was not anything made that was made. In him was life, and the life was the light of men. The light shines in the darkness, and the darkness has not overcome it...And the Word became flesh and dwelt among us, and we have seen his glory, glory as of the only Son from the Father, full of grace and truth (John 1:1-5,14).

Jesus, God's Son, is the Word made flesh. He dwelt among us. The Word of God, which hovered over the waters and creation obeyed, now walked with men. God was speaking by his Son and now we could hear him speak with our own ears. God spoke in many times and many ways, but when God spoke by his Son, Jesus, his Word was complete. There is no other phase of God speaking to us because Jesus is God's final Word.

> When we are in a crisis of faith, what we
> need to hear most is the Word of God.

This stops me in my tracks. God has spoken in his Son. Have I taken the time to listen to his voice? When was the last time I sat in prolonged silence and sought him through his Word? When we are in a crisis of faith, what we need to hear most is the Word of God. We need to hear from Jesus. Consider this:

> When I complain that I don't hear the word of God, when I feel a desire to hear the voice of God, and get frustrated that he does not speak in ways that I may crave, what am I really saying? Am I really saying that I have exhausted this final decisive Word revealed to me so fully in the New Testament? Have I really exhausted this Word? Has it become so much a part of me that it has shaped my very being and given me life and guidance? Or have I treated it lightly— skimmed it like a newspaper, dipped in like a taste tester— and then decided I wanted something different, something more? This is what I fear I am guilty of more than I wish to admit. God is calling us to hear his final decisive Word— to meditate on it and study it and memorize it and linger over it and soak in it until it saturates us to the center of our being.[3]

Oh, girls, he is speaking, but are we listening?

The Fullness of God's Glory

"He is the radiance of the glory of God and the exact imprint of his nature, and he upholds the universe by the word of his power" (Hebrews 1:3).

God has always been serious about his glory. After Moses led the Israelites out of Egypt, he went outside their camp to a tent he called "Meeting" and asked God, "'Please show me your glory'" (Exodus 33:18). God answered, "'I will make my goodness pass before you and will proclaim before you my name, "The LORD"...But,' he said, 'you cannot see my face, for man shall not see me and live'" (19-20). The Lord put Moses in a cleft of the rock and said, "'I will cover you with my hand until I have passed by. Then I will take away my hand, and you shall see my back, but my face shall not be seen'" (22-23). God's glory was more than Moses could handle and live to tell about. Later, after Moses had done everything according to God's plan, God's glory filled the temple.

> Then the cloud covered the tent of meeting, and the glory of the LORD filled the tabernacle. And Moses was not able to enter the tent of meeting because the cloud settled on it, and the glory of the LORD filled the tabernacle. Throughout all their journeys, whenever the cloud was taken up from over the tabernacle, the people of Israel would set out. But if the cloud was not taken up, then they did not set out till the day that it was taken up. For the cloud of the LORD was on the tabernacle by day, and fire was in it by night, in the sight of all the house of Israel throughout all their journeys (Exodus 40:34-38).

His glory filled the temple and Moses wasn't able to set one foot inside. Imagine what that must have been like. I am awestruck by the thought. God did not leave his people for a minute and it was his glorious presence that led them by a cloud in the day and a pillar of fire at night. This is the image the Hebrew readers had of God's glory. It is even more astounding when the author tells them Jesus perfectly reflects the majesty of God.

No more hiding in the cleft of the rock. Do you want to see the glory of God? Look to Jesus.

We could press *pause* and worship with our whole hearts right here. Nothing compares with the glory of God. But we have only just begun to see Jesus.

What the writer says next is profound. I think reading this verse in a few different Bible translations helps us grasp its meaning a bit better. And, girls, we need to do just that. Hebrews 1:3 says Jesus is:

- "The exact imprint of his nature" (ESV).
- "[The] flawless expression of the nature of God" (PHILLIPS).
- "The exact representation of His nature" (NASB).

- "The One who—imprinted with God's image, shimmer[...] with His glory..." (THE VOICE).

The Greek word used in this passage is *charakter*, which means "the instrument used for engraving or carving" and "a mark or figure burned in or stamped on, an impression."[4] When a writer during this time sent a letter, he sealed it with a bit of wax. The wax was still soft and pliable when he took a stamp or signet ring and pressed his seal, making an exact impression of his personal mark. This was the author's way of saying, "This letter has my authority. I am the one who wrote it, sealed it, and sent it." Jesus is exactly imprinted with God's image and carries all his authority. He is flawless in his perfect expression of the nature of God. Quite simply, Jesus "gives us the best picture of God we'll ever get" (2 Corinthians 4:4 MSG).

When God wanted to speak his final word, he didn't send another prophet—Israel had had plenty of those. He sent Jesus, his Son, whose glory and character perfectly reflect and precisely portray his own character. Of this divine character, Charles Spurgeon said, "The character of God is a sea, every drop of which should become a wellhead of praise for His people."[5] The character of God is a sea for us to swim in, sweet friends—an endless source for praise. What a beautiful picture to push us forward, because there is more for us to grasp.

Faithful to Hold All Things Together

As if we need more, the good just keeps getting better. Hold on, dear friend, because this next statement is like the arms of God wrapping around his daughter. Hebrews 1:3 adds a promise, saying, "And he upholds the universe by the word of his power." Jesus upholds everything and everyone. In other words, he upholds all the things, you being one of them. How does he do that? He manages and maintains the universe by his powerful, living, spoken Word.

I remember a time recently when I felt as though my own strength had vacated my entire body. I grabbed a verse a friend shared with me months before during the first few minutes after my dad suddenly passed away. It mirrors this truth found in Hebrews: "He is before all things, and in him all things hold together" (Colossians 1:17). I love how Matthew Henry wrote it best: "He upholds all things by the word of his power: he keeps the world from dissolving."

I wrote this in my book *Fresh Out of Amazing*:

> And somehow in the blur, we packed all six of us into our van and drove for two days to Indiana to be with my mom, brother, sister-in-law and other family members and friends. We mourned deeply and I kept doing the next thing I had to do, one thing at a time. A dear friend, Lisa-Jo, told me, "Stacey, the only way through is through. No matter what, you have to go through it. And you will. And God will hold you together because that is what he does. He holds everything together, and everything includes you."[6]

I promise you this is true in the moments we can't stand on our own. It's true when we don't know what is coming next. It's true even if we don't feel as though it's true. Jesus will hold you together because that is what he does. I'm living proof.

Finished the Work of Salvation

"After making purification for sins, he sat down at the right hand of the Majesty on high" (Hebrews 1:3).

Do you know that in the temple's most holy place, where the sacrifices were made on behalf of the people, absolutely no chairs were there for sitting down? Why? Because the priest's work was never finished. He was always working. There were so many people, so many sins, and so many sacrifices. How could he ever stop? But Jesus, the final Word of God, reconciled us to God by purging all our sins, once and for all. And then he did something shockingly simple and yet bold in declaration: He sat down. This shows us he entirely finished the work of our salvation. Jesus foretold this during his testimony to the Sanhedrin, a gathering of Jewish leaders including priests and scribes, before he was taken to Pilate and later crucified: "From now on the Son of Man shall be seated at the right hand of the power of God" (Luke 22:69).

Can you imagine the look on their faces when he told them this?

They must have been stunned. He knew the work of salvation would be finished. He knew his rightful seat was beside his Father in heaven. He had no doubts.

His bold confidence reminds me, ever so slightly, of our daughter Abby when she was quite small. Every time she completed a task she would throw her hands up in the air and shout, "Ta-da!" She was so proud of herself. It didn't matter what she finished. It could be dinner, a puzzle, or a toddler-sized art project. She let us know she had no doubts her project was complete. It was a ta-da moment. We were more than willing to celebrate with her and we did so several times each day.

I think the disciples must have felt like celebrating the same way when they were with Jesus after his resurrection. Mark records in his Gospel what they saw with their own eyes: "Then the Lord Jesus, after he had spoken to them, was taken up into heaven and *sat down at the right hand of God*" (Mark 16:19, emphasis mine).

This was the moment. Everything Jesus had told them was true. Oh the joy they must have felt on that day. "Thus proving himself, by the more glorious name that he has won, far greater than all the angels of God" (Hebrews 1:4 PHILLIPS).

Jesus proved himself. In doing so he has won a far more glorious name than all the angels. The salvation work is complete. Together with the disciples and the great cloud of witnesses in heaven, we can raise our hands and say, "Ta-da!" He is so worth our worship. He is worth it all.

The Transformational Power of Starting with Worship

Every other book I've written has finished with a chapter devoted to worship. I believe when we work through the hard places in our lives and we find hope and healing, worship is a beautiful and appropriate response. The book of Hebrews might be my favorite book in the Bible because it begins and finishes with worship, saying in the final chapter, "Our constant sacrifice to God should be the praise of lips that give thanks to his name" (13:15 PHILLIPS). I'm praying this is true for us as we walk together through the pages of this book as well.

As I have reflected on this first chapter of Hebrews and the boldness of the writer to start at the feet of Jesus, I was reminded of the prophet Isaiah. He started with worship too. What he described of his encounter with the Lord gives us a vivid picture of the transformational power of worship as well as a model we can apply to our own start-with-worship moment.

> In the year that King Uzziah died I saw the Lord sitting upon a throne, high and lifted up; and the train of his robe filled the temple. Above him stood the seraphim. Each had six wings: with two he covered his face, and with two he covered his feet, and with two he flew. And one called to another and said: "Holy, holy, holy is the LORD of hosts; the whole earth is full of his glory!"
>
> And the foundations of the thresholds shook at the voice of him who called, and the house was filled with smoke. And I said: "Woe is me! For I am lost; for I am a man of unclean lips, and I dwell in the midst of a people of unclean lips; for my eyes have seen the King, the LORD of hosts!"
>
> Then one of the seraphim flew to me, having in his hand a burning coal that he had taken with tongs from the altar. And he touched my mouth and said: "Behold, this has touched your lips; your guilt is taken away, and your sin atoned for."
>
> And I heard the voice of the Lord saying, "Whom shall I send, and who will go for us?" Then I said, "Here I am! Send me" (Isaiah 6:1-8).

When Isaiah caught a glimpse of the Lord in his glory, it was during the year King Uzziah died. What do you think was going on in Isaiah's heart at the time? Do you think he was grieving? Was his life in a crisis of faith—maybe a bit like yours has been of late? I think it's safe to assume Isaiah might have had a few questions for the Lord then. History tells us for most of his life King Uzziah was a good king, at least on the surface. His people grew in economy and God gave him victories in war. But at the end of his life the truth of his prideful heart was made evident. And when King Uzziah died, Isaiah, the prophet of God, was left with a people whose hearts were far from the Lord. They were a nation at a crossroads.

God chose such a moment to break through and reveal he was not a God in crisis. What Isaiah saw was the same final Word, fullness of God's glory, and rescuer we see in Hebrews chapter 1. The Lord sat high and lifted up with the train of his robe filling the temple. Did you know the robe of the priest had great significance? I didn't. My daughter told me recently a longer robe signified a priest's more glorious position. The train of our Lord's robe *filled* the temple.

I remember seeing the wedding dress Princess Diana (William and Harry's mum) wore on July 29, 1981, when she walked down the aisle toward her prince. It was glorious. Everyone was in awe of the long train trailing behind her. It went on for miles. Or seemed to. But did it fill the entire church? Not like the robe Isaiah saw. It filled the temple full of glory. Can you imagine?

While Isaiah was reflecting on the vision, he noticed the Lord was being constantly attended to in worship by a group of seraphim. The Voice Bible translation calls these angel-like beings "flaming creatures."

> Like some fiery choir, they would call back and forth continually.
>
> **Flaming Creatures:** Holy, holy, holy is the Eternal, the Commander of heavenly armies!
> The earth is filled with His glorious presence!
>
> They were so loud that the doorframes shook, and the holy house kept filling with smoke (Isaiah 6:3-4).

What he witnessed brought Isaiah low. It humbled him to the point that all he could utter was the declaration of his own uncleanliness. He was just as lost and sinful as the people he ministered to daily. He might have been the mouthpiece of God, but his own mouth was unholy in the sight of a holy God. The prophet was completely humbled in this moment of worship. A.W. Tozer put it this way:

The man who has not been humbled in the presence of
God will never be a worshiper of God at all. He may be
a church member who keeps the rules and obeys the discipline, and who tithes and goes to conference, but he'll
never be a worshiper unless he is deeply humbled.[7]

True worship deeply humbles us, just as it did Isaiah. He saw the
Lord and he knew immediately he was not worthy of the calling on his
life to serve him. How many times have we gone through the motions
of worship but not let God humble us? Tozer goes on to call this "a
humbling but delightful sense of admiring awe." To be found on our
knees at the throne of our exalted Lord is a beautiful part of our undoing, and it is a necessary work. We can join the fiery chorus and cry,
"Holy, Holy, Holy," knowing in the process we will certainly be changed
and he is worth it.

As a true worshiper, Isaiah recognized a holy God and realized his
own sin. Immediately upon Isaiah's confession, the seraphim flew to
him and touched his mouth with a burning coal taken from the altar
of the Lord, then said, "'Behold, this has touched your lips; your guilt
is taken away, and your sin atoned for'" (Isaiah 6:7). God received Isaiah's worship, restored him, and then asked, "'Whom shall I send, and
who will go for us?'" (6:8).

Isaiah couldn't respond quickly enough to the question. He didn't
look around to see who else could volunteer for the mission. He said
immediately, "Here I am! Send me" (6:8). Isaiah knew in that moment
he wanted to be the one who was sent by the Lord. In fact, I think he
pleaded with God for the opportunity with his whole heart. Can you
see the transformational power of worship at work here? Who else
could take a grieving, broken-down prophet and stir him up to the
point he begs to be sent back to the people who have rejected his every
word? Only Jesus.

Do you need to sit and receive the finished work of
Jesus today? Do you need to remember he holds you no
matter what? Take your moment, friend. Sit and receive.

I don't know why you picked up this book. I don't know what is going on in your life today. Maybe, like me, you are feeling a bit weary and worn thin. Maybe you feel sweet tears pooling in your eyes because you've caught a tiny glimpse of who Jesus is from the pages of his Word. Maybe, just maybe, it has been far too long since you let your heart simply worship at his feet. I love what my favorite worship leader, Christy Nockels, once said: "Sometimes it is an act of obedience to just sit and receive what Jesus has already done for us."[8] Do you need to sit and receive the finished work of Jesus today? Do you need to remember he holds you no matter what? Take your moment, friend. Sit and receive.

And when you have lifted your head and the question "Whom shall I send?" rises from his heart to yours, answer with a fierce determination, "Lord, send me."

Jesus will say, "Your faith has made you well. Go, beloved daughter. Go."

Fear(less)

Hebrews 2; Philippians 4:8-9

Fear had the run of my home for the entire month of February. I'm not proud of it. With my sweet eight-year-old girl tucked in bed beside me, I spent the better part of a night wrestling something much larger than I could bear alone. Body and soul depleted, sleep still evaded me. Fear took its place and settled in for a long talk.

I dozed in and out of the fog fear left in its wake and reminded myself over and over again that God was with me and he would fight for me. *He was fighting for me.* This promise in Exodus 14:14 was like a banner over me deep into the night: "The LORD will fight for you, and you have only to be silent."

My daughter had been quite ill for the past year with a chronic illness and we were deeply concerned for her health. It seemed no matter what we did, she got worse. As her health spiraled downward, so did my faith. I thought maybe I was making a little bit of headway with that four-letter word called fear, but then my daughter asked if we could talk on the way to the drugstore to pick up a few items. I said, "Of course," and we jumped into the van.

She buckled her seat belt and before we pulled out of our driveway said, "Mommy, I'm afraid. Last night I had a bad dream."

"What are you afraid of, sweetheart?"

"I don't really know. But it's big."

She didn't need to explain; I knew exactly what she was talking about. Fear is a bully and a coward simultaneously. It doesn't care if you're grown up or not quite ten years old. Fear knows how to push us around. It also knows it is powerless to do anything unless we allow it.

Our conversation in the van reminded me of one of my favorite books, *Hinds' Feet on High Places* by Hannah Hurnard. The main character's name is Much Afraid. She has a family of Fearlings who torment her day and night. The chief tormenter is her cousin, Craven Fear, who, by the way, the Fearlings want her to marry. We can see him at work both as a bully and a coward in this scene from the book:

> She shrank away from him and shook with terror and loathing. Unfortunately this was the worst thing she could have done, for it was always her obvious fear which encouraged him to continue tormenting her. If only she could have ignored him, he soon would have tired of teasing and of her company and would have wandered off to look for other prey. In all her life, however, Much Afraid had never been able to ignore Fear. Now it was absolutely beyond her power to conceal the dread she felt.
>
> Her white face and terrified eyes immediately had the effects of stimulating Craven's desire to bait her. Here she was, alone and completely in his power. He caught hold of her, and poor Much Afraid uttered one frenzied cry of terror and pain. At that moment Craven Fear loosed his grasp and cringed away.[1]

Poor girl. My heart breaks for the dear. Come to think of it, I see my strong reflection in her story every time I read it. What made the difference? Why did Craven Fear suddenly loose his grasp on Much Afraid? The story continues:

> The Shepherd had approached them unperceived and was standing beside them. One look at his stern face and flashing eyes and the stout Shepherd's cudgel grasped in his

strong, uplifted hand was more than enough for the bully. Craven Fear slunk away like a whipped cur.[2]

Do you find yourself identifying with our girl Much Afraid too? Much Afraid gave her tormenter power because she did not ignore him. He knew it and baited her all the more. She felt alone and lost to his power. But was she? When did Craven Fear loose his grip and slink away? In the presence of the Shepherd, fear had no choice but to flee: Jesus said, "I am the good shepherd. I know my own and my own know me, just as the Father knows me and I know the Father; and I lay down my life for the sheep" (John 10:14-15).

> We must return to this act of grace—the gospel—time and time again. We need to remember it. We need to rehearse it. And we need to rest in this truth.

Fear is Satan's calling card, meant to terrorize us and make us feel alone. Our Good Shepherd knows this and has already won the battle. He came to deliver a decisive blow to our greatest enemy and the weapons he uses against us. We must return to this act of grace—the gospel—time and time again. We need to remember it. We need to rehearse it. And we need to rest in this truth.

Hebrews quickly moves from worship in chapter 1 to an action point in chapter 2—to call to mind the powerful truth of the gospel. In fact, it gives us a stern warning:

> *Therefore we must pay much closer attention to what we have heard,* lest we drift away from it. For since the message declared by angels proved to be reliable, and every transgression or disobedience received a just retribution, *how shall we escape if we neglect such a great salvation?* It was declared at first by the Lord, and it was attested to us by those who heard, while God also bore witness by signs and wonders and various miracles and by gifts of the Holy Spirit distributed according to his will (2:1-4, emphasis mine).

This passage gives us a...

- warning not to neglect the gospel,
- witness to the gospel, and
- wonders and signs supporting the gospel.

What more do we need? We have wonders, we have witnesses, and we have a warning. *Don't neglect it. Don't be careless. Don't drift away.* Why would the writer be so determined that the Hebrews not neglect this message? I'll give you one guess.

Fear.

Fear showed up to boss the Hebrew believers around too. They were so afraid at this point that they were thinking of going back to the comfort of what they knew before—the law. Being Jewish wasn't exactly popular at that time, but for some being a Christ follower was proving to be deadly. The Hebrews were being persecuted, too, although not yet to the point of giving over their lives. But that sacrifice was more than a future possibility. Moving forward by faith is not easy when all you see is a trial in front of you. They were in danger of drifting away, so the writer wanted to remind them what Jesus had done for them. Matthew Henry gives us a glimpse of why the writer might have pressed hard on this subject for the Hebrews so early.

> Our minds and memories are like a leaky vessel, they do not without much care retain what is poured into them; this proceeds from corruption of our natures, the enmity and subtlety of Satan (he steals away the word), from the entanglements and snares of the world, the thorns that choke out the good seed.[3]

I think the writer knew the Hebrews needed a refresher course on the truth and power of the gospel, not merely to save them but to be the fuel they needed in their everyday lives. They were in danger of not retaining what had already been poured into them, while at the same time the Enemy was doing his level best to snatch away the Word from their hearts. Can you feel their fear doing that very thing? The same warning applies to us. If we are going to let the gospel message change our lives, we must engage with it, especially during hard times.

Warning and Wooing

As any parent would, I warn and woo my children many times in the same hour. I confess my stern warnings are sometimes followed by a hug and a cup of ice cream. I desperately want my girls to listen to my words and heed them. But they are my kids, for goodness' sake. I don't want them to remember my fierceness and forget my fondness for them.

The writer of Hebrews might have been a parent as well, because this next section of chapter 2 sounds like my scooping ice cream and loving on my girls. It seems to be a complete tangent to what he was saying before, or at least a calculated move to get them to keep listening to the message he so wanted them to grasp.

I think at this point I should say I'm really tired of calling him "The Writer of Hebrews." I wish he had a name, although I suppose it works out better for the author to not be known as Paul, John, or Peter. But I have no doubt in my heart the real author is the Lord himself. I can hear him saying these words directly to us, the church—and directly to me. He wrote it to hurting hearts in the middle of a trial who were trying to hightail it back to what felt comfortable. This book comes in like a lion for the wounded heart. Jesus is on every page.

I was wooed by this truth right in the middle of chapter 2 and the stern warning: "What is man, that you are mindful of him, or the son of man, that you care for him? (2:6).

He is *mindful* of us. He *remembers* me. He *calls* you to mind. Does that surprise you? I ask, along with Job, "What is man, that you make so much of him, and that you set your heart on him?" (Job 7:17).

You know Job, right? He was being all kinds of faithful, but when the Enemy was looking for someone to devour, God himself said, "Have you considered my servant, Job?" (Job 1:8). God recommended him for the job...so to speak.

And smack in the middle of losing it all Job found a truth you and I can cling to as well. When you are in the middle of a soul-wrenching trial, God makes much of you. He sets his heart on you. He is mindful of you. Over and over in Scripture God was mindful of his people. Think of the stories of Noah, Abraham, Isaac, Jacob, Rachel, and Hannah...to name only a few. I don't know what this truth does for your heart, but it reduces me to tears. Not the sad, I'm-in-over-my-head tears, but tears of gratitude. Thankfulness overwhelms me because Jesus is mindful of:

- The daughter who misses her daddy.
- The wife who wonders if she will ever pray enough for her husband.
- The weary mom who can't keep up with her dishes and laundry to save her life.
- The widow who cries in the shower.
- The little girl facing challenges bigger than her little body can handle.
- The broken beautiful heart who releases her will to the only One who is truly amazing.

Jesus calls that girl to mind.

> The gospel so beautifully reminds us Jesus
> is mindful of us and has been forever.

We ought to let ourselves be wooed right now by this truth. We can take a good long look at Jesus and breathe deeply. *He is mindful of us.* We are not consumed by fear. And we can carry on no matter what we are facing because of our good, good Shepherd and what he has done for us. The gospel so beautifully reminds us Jesus is mindful of us and has been forever.

The Gospel Changes Lives

Lives are changed when the gospel of Christ is proclaimed. The gospel—the good news of Jesus dying on the cross to pay for our sins and rising from the dead—changed the lives of Peter and the other remaining disciples radically. They went from being fearful hiders to bold proclaimers willing to die for their newfound faith.

The gospel spread with an unstoppable force across Jerusalem, Judea, Samaria, and ultimately the world. It is still changing lives today. How? What is the power of the gospel in action? I think the book of Hebrews gives us one of the most beautiful glimpses of this.

> Since therefore the children share in flesh and blood, he himself likewise partook of the same things, that through death he might destroy the one who has the power of death, that is, the devil, and deliver all those who through fear of death were subject to lifelong slavery (2:14-15).

Jesus shared in our humanity so that he might, through his death, defeat and destroy our enemy. In doing so he set us free from being captive to all our fears, mainly death. This fear makes us slaves. But Jesus sets us free. As Hebrews 2:10 puts it, "It only makes sense that God, by whom and for whom everything exists, would choose to bring many of us to His side by using suffering to perfect Jesus, the founder of our faith, the pioneer of our salvation" (THE VOICE). It made sense that Jesus would suffer and this would be how he would choose to bring us into a relationship with him. The King James Version says it this way: "*It became him*, for whom are all things, and by whom are all things, in bringing many sons unto glory, to make the captain of their salvation perfect through sufferings" (emphasis mine).

Suffering became him. Does that bring even more tears to your eyes? It does for me. God is telling us it was fitting for our captain to suffer. Only through suffering could he accomplish and finish the work. He deprived the devil of his influence over the children of God. He loosed us from him. He set us free from the fear of death. He released the captives. And now, having done so, he can come to the aid of those of us who are being tempted to turn back in fear. He is our captain, our shepherd, and he will surely come to our aid, just like in the story of Much Afraid. And our enemy will slink away. He has no choice.

Romans 8:32 says, "If He did not spare His own Son, but handed Him over on our account, then don't you think that He will graciously give us all things with Him?" (THE VOICE). Why would I ever need to worry or lack faith that God would go to the ends of the world on my behalf? No, the gospel reminds us that God gave it all to deliver us from the Enemy, who is dead set on devouring our hearts. The Enemy has no true power over us. This truth stirs up holy boldness.

What is the alternative to boldness? We will crouch in fear. We will live devoured and destroyed. When fear is on the warpath, you need merely to anchor your soul to the sacrifice of Jesus and plant yourself firmly in the victory he has already won on your behalf.

> That is what Hebrews does to us: it helps us to focus on the One who is already in the place of victory. We are fighting a battle already won, and that is what encourages us. When we walk in the flesh, we are fighting a battle already lost; there is no chance, no hope of victory; but when we walk in the Spirit, the battle is already won.[4]

We can't fight losing battles anymore, sweet friends. They simply don't exist.

Feeding Fear Versus Growing Peace

Do you know Jesus said "Do not fear" to his followers more than he said anything else? We are prone to feel fear. Jesus knew that about us. But, friends, we don't have to let fear rule our lives. Writer Crystal Stine said,

> Feeling fear is not a failure, friend. Feeding it is. Letting the enemy use it to build a wall of false protection around your heart only leaves you lonely and missing out on the blessings and miracles God wants us to experience. I don't want to miss out any more. I will feel fear. But it will not define me.[5]

After reading this from Crystal, I let this truth sit with my heart the better part of the day. I said, "Lord, if I don't feed fear, what should

I feed?" Almost instantly I heard him say, "Feed peace. Grow peace instead." And my mind went straight to Philippians:

> Whatever is true, whatever is honorable, whatever is just, whatever is pure, whatever is lovely, whatever is commendable, if there is any excellence, if there is anything worthy of praise, think about these things. What you have learned and received and heard and seen in me—practice these things, and the God of peace will be with you (Philippians 4:8-9).

What is truer, more honorable, purer, and more lovely than the gospel of Jesus? Nothing. Is anything more excellent and praiseworthy than the sacrifice of Jesus on our behalf? Not according to the apostle Paul, who devoted his life to sharing the gospel. His life was transformed by the gospel. He could not stop talking about it.

In the book of Ephesians, also written by Paul, he asked the believers to "pray also for me, that whenever I speak, words may be given me so that I will fearlessly make known the mystery of the gospel" (6:19 NIV). Paul wanted them to pray that he would speak boldly about the suffering of Jesus that won our salvation. He wanted them to pray that whenever he opened his mouth he would tell others death couldn't defeat Jesus—he conquered it and was raised to sit in heaven at the right hand of God. (Sound familiar?) He wanted to be fearless in proclaiming the true, honorable, pure, praiseworthy hope we all have in the captain of our salvation. I love that we can see the result of these bold prayers when Paul tells the Philippians, "Join in imitating me" (Philippians 3:17). The gospel had a firm grip on Paul's life, and it was worth imitating.

> Observe, Paul's doctrine and life were of a piece. What they saw in him was the same thing with what they heard from him. He could propose himself as well as his doctrine to their imitation. It gives a great force to what we say to others when we can appeal to what they have seen in us. And this is the way to have the God of peace with us—to keep

close to our duty to him. The Lord is with us while we are with him.[6]

Paul's life and doctrine were the same. We see no separation in what he said and what he did. His doctrine was the gospel; it changed his life and was actively at work in his life—every day.

> A gospel-gripped life grows peace and
> fear flees. It doesn't have a choice.

Even if Paul is not the author of Hebrews, his life probably had influence over the writer of the book. Paul's transformation from being a murderer of Christians to eventually a Christian martyr can only be explained by the power of the gospel. The gospel gripped Paul's life, and it must grip ours. A gospel-gripped life grows peace and fear flees. It doesn't have a choice.

This harmony is perfectly described in Hebrews 2:17-18.

> He had to become as human as His sisters and brothers so that when the time came, He could become a merciful and faithful high priest of God, called to reconcile a sinful people. Since He has also been tested by suffering, He can help us when we are tested (THE VOICE).

The gospel changed 12 men who walked with Jesus. It changed Paul, who at an earlier time in his life would just as soon have killed Jesus himself. It changed the writer of Hebrews, and it had the power to change the lives of the Hebrews as they held fast to the message, calling these truths to mind daily:

- He defeated our enemy.
- He destroyed the power of fear.
- He delivers the help we need, when we need it most.

The gospel changes us as well. Sweet friends, I know pressing forward with faith is not easy. But can you see for now, with eyes wide open at all Jesus did for us, that he is absolutely worth it?

Because he is.

Our Response and God's Glory

Whenever the gospel is preached, a response is required. Either we believe it or we don't. As followers of Christ, are we living like we believe? Has a holy boldness risen up in us as we focus on the truths found in Hebrews chapter 2?

Like the Hebrew believers, you may be facing a trial of epic proportions. Fear has probably come knocking at your door with great fervor, and you may not feel bold. But the gospel is our hope. As we live within it we are changed from glory to glory (2 Corinthians 3:18). Ultimately, though, it is not for us; it is for the glory of God.

> Understanding that I am not the ultimate end of the gospel but rather that God's glory is, actually enables me to embrace my salvation more boldly than I would otherwise dare to do. For example, when my timid heart questions why God would want to love one so sinful as I, I read the answer "to the praise of the glory of His grace." I figure, then, that my unworthiness must actually be useful to God, because it magnifies the degree to which His grace might be glorified as He lavishes His saving kindness upon me. This line of reasoning makes perfect sense to me and convinces me to embrace the gospel with greater passion so that God might glorify Himself through me, an unworthy sinner. Indeed, the more I embrace and experience the gospel, the more I delight in the worship of God, the more expressive my joy in Him becomes, the more I yearn to glorify Him in all I say and do.[7]

Can you believe our unworthiness is useful to God? It magnifies his grace. We can't drift away from this truth. We must preach it over our hearts every day. I think one of the best ways to do that is to tell him today through a declaration of his Word through prayer.

Lord, you have said:

For God so loved his children made of flesh and blood that he became one too. He was born of the same human form so that he could die and in dying he might destroy the one who had the power of death. It is the only way he could deliver those of us who are subject to the lifelong slavery of the fear of death. It was necessary so that he could be our merciful and faithful High Priest and deal with our sins once and for all.

Our part? To believe.

And *whoever* believes shall not perish under the weight of that fear. Death no longer has a claim on us. We have everlasting life because of his grace (John 3:16; Hebrews 2:14-15).

This is marvelous truth for our hearts.

Jesus, "thank you" seems so inadequate. You wore suffering because it was fitting for the captain of our salvation to do so. As our champion, you accomplished the necessary work to free us. May this gospel message never be far from our hearts. Let us pay close attention to it every day so we will not drift from it. Instead we will be changed from the inside out.

Bold and free.

All for your glory.

Amen.

Abraham to Anchors

Hebrews 6:1-20; Ephesians 1:4-5

I've been on a fiction reading binge lately. I recently devoured an entire novel in two days, neglecting truly important things like dishes and laundry. (I promise I did feed the children and kiss my husband good-bye as he headed out the door for work.) I love getting lost in the words and times of historical fiction the most. I realized recently that reading also serves to unlock my written words and to your great benefit helps them flow with some degree of elegance. In short, reading many words makes me a better writer, if not a better housekeeper.

Others of you might be like I was a few years ago: too tired to mess with make-believe stuff in books that really isn't all that important. I have fallen asleep reading countless books because I am, after all, a weary mom. I get it; I truly do. Netflix is your best friend because you can watch a story unfold while you sort socks. I promise you I do that as well. Either way, a good story is just good for the soul.

God wired us to need story. Story is what sinks down into our memory banks. Fortunately for us, God packed the Bible full of stories, only these stories are not about make-believe mythical lands or made-up creatures. As Chuck Swindoll put it, "Scripture doesn't presume to tell fairy tales. It's a book about real life."[1] The stories are about real people, many just trying to get through their everyday lives. Most of the places in the Bible can still be found on a map or reached by boat or plane. God used story to illustrate epic events like the creation of the world and the journey of the Israelites out of Egypt. We can close our eyes and visualize them because God used the exclamation point of stories throughout his Word.

Jesus understood the power of a good story as well. He was a master teller of parables with a purpose. He knew a teacher could spout off line after line of law and theology that no one would care about or begin to understand. Stories, however, caused people to lean in and listen. His style of teaching allowed him to sit down and engage with his audience in a way few, if any, rabbis were willing to do. They distanced themselves. Jesus gathered groups who hung on his every word. People sat spellbound, often forgetting to eat, some for three whole days. (There's a story about that too. You can find it in Matthew 15.)

Hebrews is a New Testament book that feels to me like it belongs in the Old Testament. Rich with history, Hebrews reaches back into the stories we might have learned as children. Hebrews doesn't just tell us; it shows us.

One of my favorite Bible characters is mentioned more than once in Hebrews. He also happens to be the first Hebrew, the father of the nation of Israel. "Abraham blazed a trail for the rest of us; his faith journey tells us about our own."[2] Now don't you want to know more?

We have talked about worship, probably my favorite topic, and I've admitted my recent battle with fear. What we need here is a story about someone who endured. We need to put flesh on it. We need to meet up with Abraham and find a little bit of us and a whole lot of Jesus. That means skipping ahead in Hebrews, but if you're okay with that, let's get started. I promise you we'll come back to the real chapter 3 of Hebrews later.

Looking Back and Moving Forward

The book of Hebrews starts out like a sermon I might have heard growing up in my tiny Baptist church in rural Indiana. We didn't have padded pews or carpet or air conditioning, but we did have Sunday school with grape juice and flannelgraphs to tell us our favorite Bible stories. Some might say this is necessary for childhood spiritual formation. Kids today would be less than amused, I'm sure. When Sunday school ended, we would file into the sanctuary to hear what our preacher had to say. Unfortunately, he didn't use flannelgraph to hold our attention like our Sunday school teacher did. Still, I would not be exaggerating when I say that most Sunday mornings involved a powerful word we were sure not to miss, even if we had dozed off in the heat on the uncomfortable pews. The beginning of the letter to the Hebrews reminds me of this, but as the writer moves along with his message, a beautiful letter of exhortation emerges. It pulls us along as well because our hearts know they need to hear more. Even when it hurts just a little bit.

Some people believe the first verse in chapter 6 is a turning point in the letter. It reads:

> Let's push on toward a more perfect understanding and move beyond just the basic teachings of the Anointed One. There's no reason to rehash the fundamentals: repenting from what you loved in your old dead lives, believing in God as our Creator and Redeemer, teaching about baptism, setting aside those called to service through the ritual laying on of hands, the coming resurrection of those who have died, and God's final judgment of all people for all time. No, we will move on toward perfection, if God wills it (6:1-3 THE VOICE).

He isn't just preaching at them. The writer desires his readers to move toward or "go on to maturity" (6:1). The problem the Hebrew congregation seemed to be experiencing was that they were edging the other way. They were more than happy to relive their spiritual childhood. The Hebrews wanted to rehash the basics and remember the good old days of Sunday school. As Warren Wiersbe said, "God had spoken in the Word but they were not faithful to obey Him."[3]

I know this to be true in my life. When God speaks I need to do what he says. If I don't move forward in obedience, I fall back; when I fall back, growth simply doesn't happen. In much the same way, you can't stand still in your faith walk either. Standing still is another way of being lazy. The maturity the writer was calling out in his readers leaves no room for laziness or retreat. He wanted them to press on. It reminds me of another exhortation found in the letter to the Philippian church:

> Not that I have already obtained this or am already perfect, but I press on to make it my own, because Christ Jesus has made me his own. Brothers, I do not consider that I have made it my own. But one thing I do: forgetting what lies behind and straining forward to what lies ahead, I press on toward the goal of the prize of the upward call of God in Christ Jesus (Philippians 3:12-14).

Guess who is a stunning example of forgetting what lies behind and straining forward to what lies ahead? Can you think of someone who pressed on even in the midst of some pretty hard days when the promise didn't seem to be coming to fruition fast enough? (Did you wonder if I was ever going to get back to Abraham? If only I had a flannelgraph right now.) But seriously, how much do I love the fact that the writer reaches back to the story of Abraham to pull the Hebrews forward by faith? He uses someone they know, someone they identify with—the father of their faith—to get them moving in the right direction.

This is how he sets up his discussion: "We want you all to continue working until the end so that you'll realize the certainty that comes with hope and not grow lazy. We want you to walk in the footsteps of the faithful who came before you, from whom you can learn to be steadfast in pursuing the promises of God" (6:11-12 THE VOICE). Abraham was the perfect choice for the turning point in this letter because he was one of the faithful who came before them and he pursued the promise of God.

The Promise of God and a Bit of Backstory

When we meet a new friend, we want to know where she comes from. We want to know about her family, and we might want to know where she got her cute pair of shoes. We really like to know the backstory, don't we? So before we dive into the part of Abraham's story mentioned in chapter 6 of Hebrews, I thought we would fill in a few answers to questions you might already be longing to know.

Scripture tells us Abram, whose name later changes to Abraham, was a descendant of Shem. Shem was one of the sons of Noah and took a ride on the ark and escaped the flood. If you follow the line of Shem you will come to Terah, who was listed as the father of Abraham. This Abraham, our guy, was married to a woman named Sarai (her name later changes to Sarah). The truly important information we glean about Sarah is that she was beautiful and barren. This is key as we move forward, because God's promise will directly involve both Sarah and Abraham. We also find out Abraham and his family left their home of Ur and began a journey to the land of Canaan. But for some reason they decided to settle in Haran instead, stopping short of their destination.

With this as the backdrop, God interrupts Abraham's life. He calls this virtually unknown idol worshiper to be a recipient of his greatest blessing—an invitation to be in a relationship with him. Abraham is part of a divine plan God set into motion before he laid the foundation of the world. I love this confirmation of how God chooses his own from Ephesians 1:4-5: "Even as he chose us in him before the foundation of the world, that we should be holy and blameless before him. In love he predestined us for adoption as sons through Jesus Christ, according to the purpose of his will." God doesn't explain his choice of Abraham for this unique relationship; he simply chooses him and tells him about it. The first mention of this calling is in Genesis chapter 12. How exciting is this when God speaks to Abraham and says,

> Abram, get up and go! Leave your country. Leave your relatives and your father's home, and travel to the land I will show you. Don't worry—I will guide you there. I have plans to make a great people from your descendants. And I am going to put a special blessing on you and cause your reputation to grow so that you will become a blessing and example to others. I will also bless those who bless you and further you in your journey, and I'll trip up those who try

to trip you along the way. Through your descendants, all
of the families of the earth will find their blessing in you
(Genesis 12:1-3 THE VOICE).

God spoke. Abraham heard. What awaited him if he obeyed?

- God would guide him there.
- God would put a special blessing on him.
- God would make him a great nation.
- God would cause his reputation to grow.
- God would bless those who blessed him.
- God would protect him.

Every bit of the promise fell back upon God. And Abraham, recognizing this was a promise to grab hold of without hesitation, did exactly
what God said. This is an extraordinary act of faith. Consider this:

> If we rewind history back far enough, we discover a time in
> which virtually no one believed in God. Civilizations wor-
> shiped many gods of their own invention, and they con-
> cocted extreme superstitions to explain the unexplainable,
> but they didn't acknowledge the existence of one true Cre-
> ator of all things. Out of this mass of theologically aimless
> humanity, one man emerged who began to proclaim what
> we might call "radical theism." The man we know today as
> Abraham not only claimed that one true Creator existed
> and that all other gods did not, but he also staked his entire
> life on this belief.[4]

It is entirely possible Abraham heard the stories of grandfather
Noah and was spurred on by such faith, but the reality of life as he knew
it was a world gone mad. It wasn't popular to believe in the one true
God, let alone follow him to the ends of the earth. But that is exactly
what he did. At the age of 75, Abraham follows God to Canaan with a
promise: "To your offspring, I will give this land" (Genesis 12:7).

Immediately you might notice a potential problem with this promise.

Abraham has a wife who is childless. At this point I often wonder what God is thinking. He doesn't always seem to choose the sharpest knives in the drawer for his missions. I mean, sure, David turned out to be a great king for the most part, and Paul was an elite, trained rabbi with wit and words to match, but what did Abraham have to offer? More than once we learn in Scripture that Abraham tried to pass his beautiful and barren wife off as his sister because he was afraid for his own life. The first time he did this it didn't work out so well, so of course he tried it again. One would think he might have learned from the error of his ways in that regard, but apparently not.

In much the same way, Abraham took matters into his own hands once more and tried to claim his promise by sleeping with and fathering a child with Sarah's slave Hagar. What might shock you is that this idea came from Sarah herself. She suggested that maybe this might make perfect sense. Abraham listened to her voice instead of to God, who had once again affirmed his promise in a stunning display of his covenant to Abraham.

> Behold, the word of the LORD came to him: "This man shall not be your heir; your very own son shall be your heir." And he brought him outside and said, "Look toward heaven, and number the stars, if you are able to number them." Then he said to him, "So shall your offspring be." And he believed the LORD, and he counted it to him as righteousness (Genesis 15:4-6).

It's key for us to know that up until this point Abraham had followed God, shown a bit of faithfulness, and fallen down more than a couple of times. He was not perfect in his obedience. During this time, as his relationship with God was deepening, he was maturing. It took over 20 years for the promise to be realized. Matthew Henry states,

> There is always an interval, and sometimes a long one, between the promise and the performance. The interval is a trying time to believers, whether they have patience to endure to the end. Those who patiently endure shall

assuredly obtain the blessedness promise, as sure as Abraham did.[5]

Romans 5:3-5 tells us this is exactly how God produces hope in our lives:

> We also celebrate in seasons of suffering because we know that when we suffer we develop endurance, which shapes our characters. When our characters are refined, we learn what it means to hope and anticipate God's goodness. And hope will never fail to satisfy our deepest need because the Holy Spirit that was given to us has flooded our hearts with God's love (THE VOICE).

Suffering. Endurance. Character. This is the order God has ordained for producing hope in our lives. Don't you wish there was an easier route? It would be awesome to grab some hope the next time you ran to the grocery store, but that isn't the way it works in God's economy. Abraham learned waiting patiently was a test of endurance. He was answering the same question the Hebrew readers were considering: *Is this faith worth it?* At the same time, God was working, developing Abraham's character. Abraham had no idea hundreds and thousands of years later readers of this letter would be called to imitate his faith. Although God hinted at it in his stargazing evening, I don't think Abraham had a clue.

Now well into his nineties with a wife a few years his junior, Abraham holds the promise of God in his arms. His son Isaac was born more than 20 years after Abraham was first called by his promise-keeping God. Always-faithful God had called him, given him land, promised an heir, and delivered on every single point flawlessly and right on time. It had nothing to do with Abraham's faithfulness, but in striking contrast, the faithfulness of God himself.

Pressing the Pause Button

You might want to press the *pause* button at this place in our chapter and let this sink into the depths of your heart. There is more to

Abraham's story and we are going to jump back into Hebrews with both feet, but this backstory is too epic to rush through.

What backstory has God been weaving in your life? Do you know everything you have ever gone through has brought you to this point? God takes your faith, no matter how small, and breathes over it as only he can. Stories like this fuel our faith in the most extraordinary way because this is the same God who is working in your life. His call may seem big, but he bears the greater side of the burden of that calling. I learned this in my own life; he doesn't need me to be amazing. As it turns out he has that covered already. When I come to him with my small offering of faith, he does more than I can imagine.

> His call may seem big, but he bears the greater side of the burden of that calling.

Recently I was listening to a podcast with Jamie Ivey and guest Shelley Giglio, cofounder of the Passion Movement. Shelley said, "You can't control what God gives you. The stewardship he hands you, he hands to uniquely you. So you don't have any control over what that is. Our part of participation is just believing. Have the faith to believe God can do what he said."[6]

I don't know what God has handed you today, this month, or this year. But I am guessing you might feel a little overwhelmed. Or maybe a lot overwhelmed. Part of moving on to maturity is growing in our belief and trusting God can do what he said.

Abraham had no control over what God handed him, but I assure you God did. He proved himself faithful over and over again. Abraham's part was to believe. As we press into the next part of this story, take a moment and whisper this prayer in the quiet of your heart: "Lord, I commit today to pursuing your promise. Show me how to be steadfast and steward well what you have handed to me." Trust me, this affirmation is important. Because it is often in this place, where we commit to be steadfast, that God allows us to be tested in the most significant way. He certainly did that in Abraham's life.

God Fulfills Both Sides of the Promise

The reason we spent an enormous amount of time in this chapter telling Abraham's backstory is because it adds such depth to the next part of the story. We are going to see a fresh maturity emerge in Abraham's life. Yet even more extraordinary will be watching how God reaffirms his promise to him by not only requiring a sacrifice, but by providing the sacrifice.

If you know anything of the story of Abraham, you know this part. God called, gave him the land of Canaan, and more importantly, gave him a son in his old age. But then God did something shocking. He asked Abraham to give him—rather, sacrifice to him—the very heir to the promise on an altar of his own making.

> Take your son, your only son Isaac whom I know you love
> deeply, and go to the land of Moriah. When you get there,
> I want you to offer Isaac to Me as a burnt offering on one
> of the mountains. I will show you which one (Genesis 22:2
> THE VOICE).

Give me your son. You know, the one you deeply love. Put your promise on the altar. Every step of this part of the story makes my mama heart ache. "God, you ask too much," I want to say. I want to step into the pages of his Word and shake Abraham and say, "How are you doing this? What do you know that my faith seems too small to comprehend?"

Abraham—sojourner; former idol worshiper; son of Terah; husband to a barren, beautiful women; father—"did as he was told" (Genesis 22:3 THE VOICE).

They walked for three days, and finally his son Isaac said, "Look, we have the fire and the wood, but where is the lamb for the burnt offering?" Abraham replied, "God will provide the lamb for the burnt offering, my son" (22:7-8 THE VOICE).

Suffering. Endurance. Character. Hope. Remember? Always in that order.

I think in that moment—as Abraham was stacking the wood, binding the boy, and raising his hand ready to relinquish his promise—his hope was fixed firmly in the truth that God was worth it. You really can't be willing to do what Abraham did and not have already answered that question in the depths of your heart. I assure you, Abraham had considered this and no longer was holding only to the basics of his faith. In endurance and with deep character refined, he was pressing on, confident in hope anchored in heavenly places.

The answer came in the final moment.

> Don't lay your hand on the boy or do anything to harm him. I know now that you respect the one True God and will be loyal to Him and follow His commands, because you were willing to give up your son, your only son, to Me.

> Abraham glanced up and saw a ram behind him with its horns caught in the thicket. He went over, dislodged the ram, and offered it up as a burnt offering in the place of his son. From that day forward, Abraham called that place, "The Eternal One will provide." Because of this, people still today say, "On the Mount of the Eternal, all will be provided" (Genesis 22:12-14 THE VOICE).

I'm short of breath as I read. The novel I mentioned earlier pales in comparison to this story. Real life is so much better, isn't it? That is as long as I'm not the one building my altars and placing my promise on it.

You want me to do *what*, Lord?

Trust you with my daughter?

Believe you are worth more than my comfort?

Give up the safety of the shore and let the waves push me closer to you?

And God draws near and reminds me that what he did for Abraham he will gladly do for me.

> When God made a promise to Abraham, since he had no one greater by whom to swear, he swore by himself, saying, "Surely I will bless you and multiply you." And thus

Abraham, having patiently waited, obtained the promise
(Hebrews 6:13-15).

Surely I will bless you. I've staked my own life on it.
Abraham's story is merely a canvas for the lavish display of God's
grace. God requires, but he also provides. I honestly think heaven just
flat-out opens up in the last few verses of Genesis 22 and gives us a holy
glimpse. I wonder if Abraham saw it. Our unchangeable God wants
to show us what all that business on Mount Moriah with Abraham
was really all about. Our promise-keeping God keeps both sides of the
covenant yes for Abraham, but in a greater way for all of us in Christ.

> We have this as a sure and steadfast anchor of the soul, a
> hope that enters into the inner place behind the curtain,
> where Jesus has gone as a forerunner on our behalf, having
> become a high priest forever after the order of Melchize-
> dek (Hebrews 6:19-20).

There it is. Our hope is anchored in heaven for us. It was this
anchored hope Abraham was looking forward to. We have a better
vantage point, my sisters. We get to look back and see it with eyes wide
open.

Hope is a person. Hope is Jesus. Hope takes my eyes off what I can
see and fixes them on what is ahead. Hope has a special place in my life.
You can imagine that anytime I see the word *hope* hiding out in Scripture I pay special attention. Since I've written extensively about hope,
I want to tell you briefly what I see about hope when I look at this particular passage.

- Hope is sure.
- Hope is steadfast, like an anchor for our souls.
- Hope goes before.
- Hope secures the promise.
- Hope gives us a purpose.
- Hope is forever.

Hope is not a personality trait of God. He has revealed this to be true about himself. God is our refuge and hope is how God is. Do you want to be mature and find the secret to enduring the trials life will surely bring your way? The answer is hope. God is encouraging our weary and worn hearts with this truth today: Hope leads us to where God is—behind the veil. This is a reference custom-made for the Hebrew readers whose very lives were centered on the temple and the work of the priests. They knew God's presence hovered behind the veil and was accessible only to the priests who entered once a year, bearing the blood of the sacrificial lamb for themselves and the people. Behind the veil was the place where reconciliation flowed. Jesus led the way as our forerunner through his death on the cross, and he invites us to follow. The law required sacrifice, and grace provided its payment once and for all. This is the gospel of hope and a true work of God.

> For the promise to Abraham and his offspring that he would be heir of the world did not come through the law but through the righteousness of faith (Romans 4:13).

You see, we get to be heirs of the promise, too, by faith in the finished work of Christ. Hope secured like an anchor; unmoving we seize it. We'd be crazy fools not to.

It Just Keeps Getting Better

> "So come on, let's leave the preschool fingerpainting exercises on Christ and get on with the grand work of art. Grow up in Christ. The basic foundational truths are in place: turning your back on 'salvation by self-help' and turning in trust toward God" (Hebrews 6:1 MSG).

When my oldest daughter, Emma, was three years old, we moved from Indiana to Central Florida. We didn't happen to mention the fact that the famous mouse and his theme park were about 20 minutes from our doorstep. In our defense, as young parents we were tight on funds and I was about eight weeks out from having her baby sister, Abby. We had our reasons for withholding this information from her.

Several months after we moved into our home and were adjusting to life as a family of four, Emma came bursting into the kitchen while I was stirring my cup of coffee.

"Mom! Mom! Did you know Disney World is *in* Florida?" She declared this life-changing news with great excitement.

"Really," I said, stalling. "Is that so?"

"We should go there because we live in Florida," she declared. This made perfect sense to her.

Later that year we decided to brave our way down to the tourist corridor of our town. We didn't have tickets to "The World," so we settled for a foreshadowing called, at that time, Downtown Disney. It sufficed for our precocious girl. She was delighted by the music, the larger-than-life Disney Store, the sweet-smelling treats, and the tiny tot-sized carousel. She assumed this must be Disney World, and we didn't correct her (I know, stellar parenting move). She chattered on and on all day and the next week about her new favorite destination. "When can we go again? I want to go to Disney," she would plead. For that year and much of the next, whenever we could break away from all the busy of resettling in our new town with new jobs and a new baby, we went to Emma's Disney.

A year or so later we met more than a few lovely people at our church who worked at the real, bona fide Disney World. They graciously shared their complimentary friends and family tickets with us. We couldn't wait to experience it with our girls. I am not exaggerating one bit when I tell you Emma's heart burst with excitement when she saw the castle in the Magic Kingdom in all its glory and met her first live princess. She was completely enchanted by it all. We were too. Disney, of course, does it best. I cried hot tears as I watched the wonder of her heart expressed on her sweet face. We had the best day ever.

We have since returned to the real Disney World many times over the past 13 years. We even sprung for season passes one year to take advantage of all the parks have to offer for our sweet girl crew. We kind of love that place and its magic. We have also returned to Downtown Disney. Emma laughs at our gentle reminder that for a long while she thought this was Disney World. "How did I think that? Disney World is so much better. There simply is no comparison."

> Choose to go on with Jesus and it will be difficult at times. But we have an anchor of hope that holds and a promise that pulls us forward.

I think you see where I'm going with this story. Maturity in Christ means we leave behind our preschool ways and move on to let him paint the grand work of art in our lives. Oh, we could stay in the Downtown Disney of our faith, so to speak, and be content. But once we catch a glimpse of the real, the truth, the hope we have in Jesus—why would we ever go back? Why would we not want to press on in maturity toward truth? I'm not saying it will be easy. Choose to go on with Jesus and it will be difficult at times. Suffering. Endurance. Character. This is God's classroom and it produces hope. But we have an anchor of hope that holds and a promise that pulls us forward.

> Hope will never fail to satisfy our deepest need because the Holy Spirit that was given to us has flooded our hearts with God's love (Romans 5:5 THE VOICE).

Let us go on, then, to maturity. Oh, my sweet friends, it is better and it is worth it.

The Word

Hebrews 4:12-16; Deuteronomy 32:45-47

I think I speak for most parents and grandparents when I say school presentations are equal parts triumphant and tedious. The triumphant parts include our own tiny people who have worked hard on their lines and songs. Like me, you have probably mustered up costumes of grandeur on their behalf, even begging the people at Party City to scour the backroom for the perfect piece for your princess. You paid way more money for it than you planned to spend, but the smile on her face made it worthwhile. She was a shining beacon on stage. You recorded it and excessively shared pictures online because you are that parent. We all are.

The tedious part comes into play because out of the longest 60 minutes of your life, your precious shines only for 2.3 seconds. Every other proud mom, dad, grandma, and grandpa has their own star to make over, so you sit and wait during their moments, trying not to look as though you're planning dinner for the next month, making your grocery list on your smartphone.

You Can't Fight a Battle When You're Thirsty

This was me a few months ago. During our spring school performance, I was marking time in my seat, praying the minutes might supernaturally tick by a bit faster than God ordains them. Having applauded my own kindergarten pilgrim girl, I was ready to be acting on my now-made grocery list when one of the other classes began a short play about a woman turned folk legend from the Revolutionary War. Her name was Molly Pitcher. At least that's what they all started calling a woman named Mary who was the wife of a barber turned soldier for the Continental Army. During the Battle of Monmouth in Freehold, New Jersey, on June 28, 1778, she made repeated trips to the nearby watering hole to fill pitchers of water for the soldiers. She walked tirelessly around the battlefield offering cold drinks to battle-weary men. Legend also tells us when her husband was injured during the battle, she took over his cannon duties. Molly Pitcher was also a gunner. She got the job done.

Obviously, I looked up from planning my grocery list during this portion of the school presentation. It was almost as if God had tapped me on the shoulder to make sure I was paying close attention as a sweet third grader in continental dress delivered her one line: "You can't fight a battle if you are thirsty." I was stunned. Right there in the middle of the third- and fourth-grade Revolutionary War tribute God spoke to me. His own words echoed in my heart from a previous study of his Word:

> Jesus said to her, "Everyone who drinks of this water will be thirsty again, but whoever drinks of the water that I will give him will never be thirsty again. The water that I will give him will become in him a spring of water welling up to eternal life" (John 4:13-14).

This truth was powerfully joined to another verse, reminding me of the power of God's Word.

> Husbands, you must love your wives so deeply, purely, and sacrificially that we can understand it only when we compare it to the love the Anointed One has for His bride, the church. We know He gave Himself up completely to make her His own, washing her clean of all her impurity with

water and the powerful presence of His word (Ephesians 5:25-26 THE VOICE).

God's Word quenches the spiritual thirst in our hearts. It washes us clean and shows us his radical love for his bride, the church. I think the writer of Hebrews was looking at a battle-weary group of believers and wanted to hold out a water-filled weapon they needed in their arsenal. They could not fight the battle thirsty. They needed to drink deep from the well. He wanted them to know God's Word does something to us, in us, and through us. But first they would have to pay attention to it.

If I've Told You Once, I've Told You Five Times

When something is important, you repeat it. In my house you'll hear me say over and over again, "Stop running." "Put your dishes in the sink." "Turn down the volume on the television." And my personal favorite, "Walk the dog." These aren't hard things to remember, but for some reason my girls have selective memory. Of course, we have repeated conversations about spiritual truths as well. My girls know without a doubt that we are going to talk about God's Word and pray a little or a lot each day. Although we do have times of purposeful study, we tend to talk about things along the way in the spirit of Deuteronomy 6.

Mostly, we talk while I'm driving them to all the places they need to be. Because after all these years of mothering I have come to realize what I truly am is a professional driver. I'm also a snack giver. It would seem as well that my best moments are while driving and dispensing snacks. I mean, this is multitasking at its best when you can navigate traffic and dig in your oversized purse for fish-shaped cheddar crackers. During these winning moments of mothering, my girls might cringe when I accidently (or rather purposely) repeat a story with spiritual significance, starting with the phrase "When I was younger." They have no qualms about telling me they've heard it before, many times. You should know, I have no qualms in ignoring them and telling them anyway.

The writer of Hebrews didn't tell his readers once to pay attention to the Word and the One speaking it; he mentioned it over and over again.

- Hebrews 2:1: "Therefore we must pay much closer attention to what we have heard, lest we drift away from it." (They have heard the Word spoken already.)

- Hebrews 3:1: "Consider Jesus, the apostle...of our confession." (Apostle = the one who speaks the Word.)

- Hebrews 3:12: "Take care, brothers, lest there be in any of you an evil, unbelieving heart." (A heart not hearing and believing the Word.)

- Hebrews 3:15: "Today, if you hear his voice, do not harden your hearts." (His voice = the Word.)

- Hebrews 4:2: "Good news came to us just as to them, but the message they heard did not benefit them, because they were not united by faith with those who listened." (The Word benefits us when combined with faith.)

Building throughout the first few chapters, he was bringing to light the centrality of the Word of God in the life of every believer. They needed this repetition because, apparently, they had selective memory, much like my daughters. They might have rolled their eyes a time or two, because what was at stake for them was their maturity. The writer also felt it was necessary to bring up the topic once again in chapter 5 and chapter 6. I think he must have had a bee in his bonnet about the matter. I love what Warren Wiersbe says about this.

> Our relationship to the Word of God determines our spiritual maturity. The people had drifted from the Word (2:1-3), doubted the Word (Chaps 3-4), and become dull toward the Word. They had not mixed the Word with faith (4:2) and practiced it in their daily lives (5:14)...instead of going forward (6:1) they were going backward.[1]

Maturity and moving forward sound similar to what we talked about in the last chapter about Abraham. You have already seen what happened in his life when he drifted from the word God spoke to him and he doubted. When he mixed the word of God with faith, he moved forward and spiritual maturity was on glorious display in his life.

I would like to skip the parts of my story when I've drifted, doubted, and grown dull to the Word of God. I want to heed the warnings and exhortations of the writer of Hebrews once and for all. I want to be found paying attention, considering, and exchanging my unbelieving heart for a faith that endures. God has not left us on our own. To help us in our own unbelief we have the living Word of God. Gratefully, in Hebrews 4:12 we have one of the most visually stunning verses in the Bible. It tells us what the Word of God is and what it does.

> The word of God is living and active, sharper than any two-edged sword, piercing to the division of soul and of spirit, of joints and of marrow, and discerning the thoughts and intentions of the heart.

The Word of God Is...
Living

You may know I have an almost nerd-like affection for the study of words. I get downright giddy over dictionaries. Don't get me started on my crush on Webster's 1828 dictionary. I hope you can put up with me for a moment as we dig a little deeper into the individual words that make up this verse. I know we can get bogged down in many details, but if you humor me for a moment or two, I think this verse will forever be engrained in your mind as it is for me.

The word *word*, or *logos* in the Greek, means "a word, uttered by a living voice, embodies a concept or idea, what someone has said, the sayings of God."[2] If you want to completely geek out with me, you will love to know *logos* was first used by a Greek philosopher named Heraclitus around 600 BC to designate the divine reason or plan that coordinates a changing universe. The Greeks, you see, didn't have any trouble believing their gods, and our God spoke with real words. Words could be divinely wrought and they often were.

The word *living*, or *quick* as some Bible translations use, is the Greek word *zaō*. It means "to live, breathe, be among the living (not lifeless, not dead), to have true life and be worthy of the name, active, blessed, endless in the kingdom of God."[3]

> When we come to the Word of God we need to know it is not like any other book. It is breathing, endless, and has true life apart from us.

The writer was basically saying, by putting *logos* and *zaō* together, "the living word is living." Was he repeating himself on purpose? Perhaps he was. Maybe he was simply blessed to have the repertoire of Greek language at his disposal. Should we have any doubt what he is saying is truth? When we come to the Word of God we need to know it is not like any other book. It is breathing, endless, and has true life apart from us. I like what R.C. Sproul once said about this.

> When I was hired to teach the Scriptures in required Bible courses at a Christian college, the president of the institution phoned me and said, "We need someone young and exciting, someone with a dynamic method who will be able to 'make the Bible come alive.'" I had to force myself to swallow my words. I wanted to say, "You want me to make the Bible come alive? I didn't know that it had died. In fact, I never even heard that it was ill. Who was the attending physician at the Bible's demise?" No, I can't make the Bible come alive for anyone. The Bible is already alive. It makes me come alive.[4]

> It is not your job to make the Word of God come alive. The living Word of God is living.

My friend, let the tremendous grace of the living Word fall fresh on you right here. Of everything you have to do today, it is not your job to make the Word of God come alive. You may have to wash dishes, tackle the laundry pile, and make a trip to the grocery store. Maybe you need to do those things again tomorrow. But you don't have to sit in front of God's Word and hope it comes alive. The living Word of God is living. Believe it and let it bring life to your weary heart.

Active (Powerful)

Sometimes the Greek word gives us a quick clue as to what it means in English. The word used here is *energēs*. Have you ever considered God's Word as possessing powerful energy? God's Word is not still. It has magnificent power. This reminds me of the first chapter of Genesis when God spoke the world into being. Just as his word empowered and brought the world into existence, it is moving powerfully in our lives as well. The Voice translation of the first part of Hebrews 4:12 says, "The word of God, you see, is alive and moving." A note under the verse adds by way of commentary, "By God's word, everything finds a rhythm, a place. It fills, empowers, enlivens, and redeems us." God's Word breathed out gives cadence to our lives and sets them firmly in place. His Word moves us powerfully toward redemption. Can your heart take more? Well, hold on, my friend, because of course it just keeps getting better.

Sharper (Than Any Two-Edged Sword)

The beauty and selection of the word used by the writer becomes crystal clear when you compare it to another word he could have chosen. *Tomos* (used here) means "sharper," as if able to cut by a single stroke.[5] *Koptō* also means to cut, but this type of cutting is more akin to our word *hack* or *chop*.[6] *Tomos* is more decisive. It means a single swift stroke is all that's needed to cut to the quick. God's Word does not need repeated blows as a single-edged sword might require.

> It is effective and efficient.
> It is sharper than any two-edged sword.

It cuts both ways.
It is the sword of the Spirit (Ephesians 6:17).
It is the two-edged sword that comes out of the mouth of Christ (Revelation 1:16).
It is sharper than any two-edged sword, *for it will enter where no sword can and make a more critical dissection*: It pierces to the dividing asunder of the soul and the spirit (emphasis mine).[7]

God's living, moving Word goes where no other weapon can—straight to the most critical point with surgical precision. What does it do once it is there in this secret place of our hearts?

This is no fluffy interchange between my heart and God's Word. If I have any sin secretly hidden where my soul and spirit meet, you can believe God's Word will find it.

The Word of God Does

The living, active Word of God does something to us and within us. First, with quick and decisive work, it exposes us and "strikes through to the place where soul and spirit meet, to the innermost intimacies of a man's being: It exposes the very thoughts and motives of man's heart" (Hebrews 4:12 PHILLIPS). This is no fluffy interchange between my heart and God's Word. If I have any sin secretly hidden where my soul and spirit meet, you can believe God's Word will find it. When I believe a paralyzing lie from the Enemy, God's Word will cut it down meticulously. His sword divides and destroys anything in disagreement with truth. And just to make sure we are clear on the matter, the writer goes on to state unapologetically, "No creature can hide from God; God sees all. Everyone and everything is exposed, open for His inspection; and He's the One we will have to explain ourselves to" (Hebrews 4:13 THE VOICE).

> Unveiled and laid bare by God's Word, I'm an
> open book. It reads me as much as I read it.

I've become pretty skilled over the years at hiding from people all around me. I have at times fooled them for weeks and years on end that I have it all together. I have even let pride enter my life and find a home in my heart, thinking I could do everything in my own strength. But the minute I choose to give God's Word the access it so desperately seeks to my heart, everything is exposed. Unveiled and laid bare by God's Word, I'm an open book. It reads me as much as I read it.

> Thankfully, what God exposes and
> inspects, he resurrects and revives.

Remember I said God's Word does something *to* us? It also does something *in* us. Thankfully, what God exposes and inspects, he resurrects and revives. His desire is to cure my unbelief and keep me (and you) from sinning. He doesn't make quick work of our hearts merely to wound us. His intention is to heal us and lead us to his mercy:

> Since then we have a Great High Priest who has passed through the heavens, Jesus, the Son of God, let us hold fast our confession. For we do not have a high priest who is unable to sympathize with our weaknesses, but one who in every respect has been tempted as we are, yet without sin. Let us then with confidence draw near to the throne of grace, that we may receive mercy and find grace to help in time of need (Hebrews 4:14-16).

Take heart, sister. God does not leave us unveiled and laid bare for long. Most importantly, he does not leave us alone. We have this wonderful provision, the same one who offered living water to the woman spiritually dying of thirst by the side of a fountain, acting as our Great High Priest and mediator. He himself sits on the throne we are bid to come to and drink deeply from. And what our hearts need most, he pours out endlessly. As I wrote in my book *Fresh Out of Amazing*...

> The invitation here is simply to come to the throne of grace and receive what we need. Of course, it's hard to receive anything before you are fresh out of amazing. If you don't have a need, you won't come. But when you are emptied, when you're aware of all the places you're lacking, when you're weak and weary, you can more easily give yourself permission to come. And you need to come.
>
> Aligning my life with this truth looks like the act of coming to God's throne and receiving his grace. I need to plant myself front and center at the throne of grace and gaze upon Jesus. It is a habit I am slowly learning. I'm so grateful he is a gentle and patient teacher.[8]

Time and time again when I have been weak and weary, God has used his Word to heal my heart. This was true that day years ago when I showed up to study the book of Hebrews for the first time. Not one time in my life have I come seeking to be filled up only to be denied by God. I think this is why I can't stop telling women about my love for God's Word.

If you ever hear me speak or read anything else I've written, you'll probably come to a part much like this chapter, where I sound a bit like a broken record. It just matters that much. I will always do my best to leave you with the encouragement to be a woman who sits at the feet of Jesus and receives his mercy through engaging with his powerful Word. I can't stop, and I won't stop. I spent years treating God's Word as an accessory I carried to church or pulled out to write a Bible verse on a note for a friend. Until I hit rock bottom and God used it to put the pieces of my heart back together I did not realize his Word is so much more than a crutch. It's a sword. I wanted to be a woman who knew how to use it once and for all. I think you, since we are now officially girlfriends, will not be surprised I want the same for you.

As If Your *Life* Depended on It

I met my friend Robin in 1989 at Indiana University when I crashed her Bible study. I guess showing up to a Bible study unannounced is not really the same thing as coming to a party without an invitation. Still, it was probably one of the boldest things I have ever done. They had been meeting for weeks when I arrived with Mary, a girl I barely knew who lived on my dormitory floor. I was lost on that Big Ten campus in a sea of people. I knew in my heart I needed to find a group of girlfriends who loved Jesus—and fast.

I remember that first night as if it were yesterday. I was gripping my black paperback NIV Student Bible as though it were a shield, afraid these girls might think I was small and uninteresting. Instead they opened their circle and ultimately their hearts wide as we bonded over our new life as college students and dived deep into the pages of God's Word. That one brave step changed the course of my life forever.

Last week, Robin arrived a few miles from my front door on vacation. I drove over to the beach condo she was staying in, and we parked our two chairs right in front of the water and watched as her boys dived in and out of the surf and two of my girls played in the sand as mermaids. We quickly talked about life and friends, and then we landed on the one subject that has bonded our lives since that first day in 1989—God's Word. It sure makes my heart smile to know that when I crashed her Bible study, God knew we'd still be talking about his Word three decades later. He planned it that way and I'm so humbled by that. As we shared what God has been teaching us, Robin reminded me of a passage from Deuteronomy:

> When Moses had finished speaking all these words to all Israel, he said to them, "Take to heart all the words by which I am warning you today, that you may command them to your children, that they may be careful to do all the words of this law. For it is no empty word for you, but your very life, and by this word you shall live long in the land that you are going over the Jordan to possess" (32:45-47).

The last words of Moses pertained to the Word of God. He was telling Israel they needed to be careful to do all that God had said as though their lives depended on it. God's Word held life and blessing. It is the same for us today. His Word has not ceased being life-giving. We can come to it every day as though *our* lives depend on it, because they do.

As I've thought long and prayed hard, I've decided it would be a good idea for me to give you a tool for studying the Word on your own. Now, let me say many great tools are out there for Bible study. This is not the only tool available. But, as a girlfriend, I think I would be remiss for not handing you something you could use to help you grow in your walk with God and love for his Word. This is something you can use in your personal Bible study or with friends.

LIFE Bible Study Method

L—Listen to God's Word

I—Investigate

F—Face-to-Face

E—Experience in Real Life

L—Listen to God's Word

When we come to a passage from the Bible—a verse, a chapter, or an entire book—we need to listen to the words. My advice is to read the passage several times. I like to read it in different translations as well. There is no time frame for this. Just read and enjoy the words.

In addition to reading the words, I like to write them. You can do this a number of different ways. When I write through a passage I use a loose form of diagramming. Mind you, I don't pull out my grammar books and make sure it's perfect. I simply diagram it in a way that helps the heart of the verse or passage pop out.

Another way of writing it is to put it into your own words. A Bible teacher told me one time that if you can say it in your own words, it will stick better. Feel free to put your written words in a fun, hard-copy journal or, like me, you might prefer to put them in a note-taking program on your computer. The bottom line for me is that reading Scripture several times and then writing it helps me to listen better and hear what God is saying to my heart. It's a perfect first step.

I—Investigate

Once you've spent some time familiarizing yourself with the passage you're studying, it's time to dig into the text. If listening is akin to stepping back and looking at the bigger picture, investigating involves zooming in and looking for details and connections. A simple study Bible and dictionary—and if you are tech savvy, an internet connection—are really all you need. I also pay special attention during the investigation phase to key words. A key word is a word in the text that is either important or repeated. Maybe as you read through the text you notice a theme or word used again and again. My advice to you is to chase down that word. Look it up in the dictionary and make sure you know what it means. If you are like me, you may want to uncover the writer's meaning with a basic Hebrew (Old Testament) or Greek (New Testament) word study based on which book of the Bible you're studying.

Because context is important, you'll want to also know what comes before and after the passage as well as what kind of writing it is. Many Bibles' individual book introductions are filled with great background information. It is perfectly fine to start there and build out on your own.

You might also use this time to look for other verses in Scripture that form a connection with this passage. This is called a cross-reference. Most basic study Bibles will list these at the bottom of the page. Because the best interpreter of a passage of Scripture is another passage from Scripture, it's good to make note of these at this time. Just list them, look them up, and note anything that helps you understand or supports your current passage.

You can spend as much time here as you like. You better believe I love a good word chase and digging for connections. I think this is where so many lightbulb moments happen for me. You know, when you get so excited you say, "Wow, I had no idea!" God continually encourages my heart as I look at the depth of meaning in his Word.

> When we open God's Word we come
> face-to-face with him.

F—Face-to-Face

Remember how when Isaiah came face-to-face with God his response was to fall on his face and worship? Friends, when we open God's Word we come face-to-face with him. My pastor, David Uth, tells us the Bible is the only book you read where the author actually shows up. When we dive deep into his Holy Word, he meets us on the page and in our hearts. More than a few times tears have come to my eyes as I've been studying. I am moved by what I'm reading.

Sometimes—many times—I'm convicted of sin in my life and I know I need to stop right then and tell God I'm sorry for it. Other times I want to raise my hands to praise him for the specific and swift encouragement he has just laid on my heart. He is just so good to us. I can't imagine creating a Bible study method that didn't encourage you to come to your Savior with gratitude, worship, and prayerful conversations. This is our time to tell him what is in our hearts. Tell him. Worship from the deepest parts of your soul. Sing. Write it down. Sit with silent adorations. Tell him, friends. Tell him.

> Worship from the deepest parts of your
> soul. Sing. Write it down. Sit with silent
> adorations. Tell him, friends. Tell him.

E—Experience in Real Life

As we read and study God's Word, it changes and matures us. It is absolutely awesome if you have a plan to study God's Word. It is better for you to be moved to worship as you do. But if the truth you encounter there doesn't make an impact on your everyday life and make you more like Jesus, you have missed a large portion of the point. Make a commitment to allow the living and active Word of God to do what it was designed to do.

Personally, living out God's Word in real life means I need to dwell on the words I'm reading. I may try to memorize a verse or two to let the passage I've been studying stick with me for a while. It always helps me to talk about it with another person, and of course, to write about it.

> The living Word of God is moving; we
> need to follow where it leads.

After I've saturated my heart with the passage, I need to take note of what action is needed. Now, the action is not always big and bold. Sometimes it's simply using kinder words with my girls or looking for opportunities to serve others as I go about my day. Other times God gets all up in my business and calls me out to speak a word to others I wouldn't dream of saying on my own. It varies. But in the depth of my heart, I know when God is moving me to take action on a truth he has revealed. The living Word of God is moving; we need to follow where it leads.

A Final Word on the Word

I'm sitting in my local office, Panera, wishing you were sitting across from me so I could make firm eye contact with you. I'd love to know if you are tracking with me or wishing I would just quit meddling. If my words fall short, don't miss this impassioned plea from an old man who took a million or so slaves out of Egypt and brought them through a 40-year walk in the wilderness: "For it is no empty word for you, but your very life" (Deuteronomy 32:47).

The Word is your very life, sweet girl. And whether you move forward or fall back, your maturity in Christ depends on it. The Word is also a love letter for your heart on the hard days when you would rather quit. It will be the sword in your hand when you need to fight. Quite simply, it's the voice of the one who was willing to become like you so you could become like him. He is the one who sits on the throne but left the glory of heaven to save you.

> God made very sure that we could understand who he is, what he is like, and what he wants for us and what he wants from us. He did this by sending his Son, Jesus. Now we don't have just the written Word, we have the Living Word—a real person. When people watched Jesus, they were seeing God.[9]

It is a living Word. His name is Jesus. He is speaking. Are you listening?

Your Great High Priest

Hebrews 5:1-10; Hebrews 7:1–8:9; John 17

One of my favorite activities is studying God's Word with a small group of committed women of faith. Time around a table with women who passionately pursue God has not only been a gift—it has transformed my heart. The sweetest relationships have happened life-on-life, sitting with our worn-out copies of the Word of God between us. Several years ago I was blessed to be part of a group that met every Monday for three years. We dragged our kids into our cars, brought bagels and coffee, and fought traffic to carve out two hours together at the beginning of our week. That effort was worth it because there we learned to become more like Jesus.

One of the women sitting at the table was my good friend Melanie. I knew no matter what part of God's Word we were studying that week, she would come to the table having let it settled into the deep places of her heart. As a group, whenever we were at a point of tension where learning becomes life, she would often say to us, "Once you know the truth, you are responsible for it." At least four of us would bury our heads on our Bibles and say, "We knew you were going to say that, Mel." We also knew she was right, and praise God, she was bold enough to say it. You see, we couldn't run from the truth staring us straight in the face. Melanie, in her seasoned teacher-like voice, became the voice in my own head every time I wanted to glance past a truth that might be hard to understand or act on.

> Once you know the truth, you are responsible for it.

Now, ten years later, that voice is still there and I speak it aloud when I want to run the other direction. Doing hard things is a mark of maturity. And since we just settled that we want to be mature women a couple of chapters back, I think it's time for me to let Melanie's words remind you that we can't go back to the days when we could live as though we didn't know. Girlfriend to girlfriend, I need to tell you this as well: Once you know the truth, you are responsible for it. The truth we have gleaned so far in the book of Hebrews is a treasure you can always return to, and you now have responsibility to act. You might think what you've learned so far is more than enough to last you a long time, thank you very much. But please, do not stop reading. Look forward with me to what we are about to uncover.

I say all this because I have a feeling when you saw the title of this chapter you thought you might just skip a few pages ahead. You wondered, *Do I really need this chapter right here? What in the world is a Great High Priest? Can we jump ahead to Hebrews 11 and sing "How Great Is Our God"?* You could do that, for sure, and no one would really know the difference. But if you want to find Christ in Hebrews, you need to wade into this part of the text with me. A large part of Hebrews deals with this theme, and the writer thoroughly discusses it throughout the book. He didn't sidestep it, and neither should we. In fact, the writer gave this fair warning in Hebrews 5:11-14:

> About this we have much to say, and it is hard to explain, since you have become dull of hearing. For though by this time you ought to be teachers, you need someone to teach you again the basic principles of the oracles of God. You need milk, not solid food, for everyone who lives on milk is unskilled in the word of righteousness, since he is a child. But solid food is for the mature, for those who have their

powers of discernment trained by constant practice to distinguish good from evil.

This subject is definitely solid food. We don't want to be accused of being a lazy listener, do we? Is it hard for you to understand? It is for me too. But this is the maturity we've been talking about. The Hebrews weren't too sure. They wanted to fall back on what they knew before, hence the strong warning. I love that the writer doesn't water down his message. He calls them upward and onward. We will not do anything different. Take heart, my sweet friend. Though it is hard, sweet mercy is here as well. Let's press on to know this truth. I think this might just be the one that makes the deepest mark in your heart. I'm praying that's true.

> From the beginning of time, God's heart beat for us
> with reconciliation and relationship in mind.

Everyone Needs a Great High Priest

From the beginning of time, God's heart beat for us with reconciliation and relationship in mind. But as you probably know, left to our own resolve we tend to destroy relationships at breakneck speed. Adam and Eve certainly did, and before we go about tossing stones their way, we should admit we are no different in the depths of our sinful hearts. To that end God provided a minister to act as a mediator between our brokenness and his holiness. We needed it in the worst possible way.

> Remember what I said earlier about the role of the high priest, even the ones chosen by human beings? The job of every high priest is reconciliation: approaching God on behalf of others and offering Him gifts and sacrifices to repair the damage caused by our sins against God and each other (Hebrews 5:1 THE VOICE).

Simply put, the job of the high priest was reconciliation. He was appointed and anointed by God to offer sacrifices for the sins of the people against God. Something was broken and his job was to fix it. God instituted, by his grace, a provision for the restitution of the ever-present sins of the people. "The priest was central to the order of worship because he was the one designated to bring the offerings to the Lord on behalf of the people. Their sins could not be forgiven without his intercession."[1] You can read in great detail about the many sacrifices the high priest offered on behalf of the people in the book of Leviticus. You can put a bookmark right here in Hebrews and turn back to this Old Testament book and spend as much time as you need walking through what our Hebrew readers knew by heart.

Now, if you are like me, you are not one to spend days and weeks in the book of Leviticus. When I think about my love for the Word of God I feel as though I need to offer a disclaimer: "When I get to heaven I'm going to apologize for falling asleep while reading the book of Numbers and avoiding the book of Leviticus." Y'all, Leviticus is hard to read. I get it. Let me cut through much of it for our personal study today by pointing out these verses in regard to the first high priest. Aaron, the brother of Moses, was to make many different types of offerings for the people, but one had special significance. It was called a sin offering and was made on behalf of the people and also himself. You see, he wasn't exempt from the sin offering.

> If the person anointed as priest commits a sin, he brings guilt on the people and they suffer the consequences. So the priest must offer the most valuable animal—an unblemished, young bull—to Me as a purification offering for sin. He must bring the bull to the entrance of the congregation tent, place his hand on the bull's head, and slaughter it in My presence (Leviticus 4:3-4 THE VOICE).

Why all the fuss?

> Sin is serious business; it destroys one's relationship with God and can even endanger entire communities. So sin must be dealt with seriously. God provides a process whereby sin may be forgiven and guilt may be set aside. It

begins with admitting you are wrong and then following
the requisite sacrifices.[2]

In Hebrews 9:22 we learn, "Indeed, under the law almost everything is purified with blood, and without the shedding of blood there
is no forgiveness of sins." The high priest was willing to get dirty on
behalf of his people and his own heart before a living and holy God. It
was a bloody mess of a job. And with so many people and so many different types of offerings (other than the sin offering), he worked tirelessly, day in and day out.

Rather oddly, this reminds me of the commercial with the Dunkin'
Donuts manager years ago. Every day he would rise in the wee small
hours of the morning and stumble through his routine, saying, "Time
to make the donuts. Time to make the donuts." This worker pro-
pelled himself along when he'd rather be in bed. It was his job to make
sure the donuts were made when the customers walked into his store
many hours later. His job required sacrifice, and he was willing to do it
because he was the Dunkin' Donuts Man and it was time to make the
donuts. Every day, come rain or come shine.

I'm not suggesting the high priest motivated himself every morning by reciting a little chant, "Time to offer some sacrifices." But something pushed him along every day to be the mediator between God
and the people. It had to, because this was no cushy desk job. The sins
of the people were not to be taken lightly. I think we can find a key in
the next couple of verses in the book of Hebrews.

> He can deal gently with the ignorant and wayward, since
> he himself is beset with weakness. Because of this he is
> obligated to offer sacrifice for his own sins just as he does
> for those of the people. And no one takes this honor for
> himself, but only when called by God, just as Aaron was
> (Hebrews 5:2-4).

The high priest had compassion on the people. He understood their
weaknesses because he had his own to deal with. I think his heart bent
toward others with kindness and grace, and he was well aware of his

own need for them. This was part of his qualification and made him worthy of the calling. The people didn't need a harsh law man; they needed a kind and gracious high priest who opened wide his arms and was a safe place to pour out their hearts.

We get a glimpse of this in the beautiful story of Hannah in the book of 1 Samuel. Where did she go when she felt as though her dreams had died and she was at the very end of herself? She went to the temple. She cried out to God and the high priest Eli was sitting nearby. Although he initially mistook her for being drunk, she appealed to him out of the depths of her heart and he said: "'Go in peace, and the God of Israel grant your petition that you have made to him.' And she said, 'Let your servant find favor in your eyes.' Then the woman went her way and ate, and her face was no longer sad" (1 Samuel 1:17-18). He blessed her and sent her in peace and she was no longer sad.

Don't we all need that at some point in our lives? I need it almost daily. I love what Charles Spurgeon said of this interaction: "It is his [the high priest's] nature to sympathize with the aching heart, but he cannot be compassionate to those who have no suffering and no need. The heart of compassion seeks misery, looks for sorrow, and is drawn towards despondency—for there it can exercise its gracious mission to the full."[3] The high priest looked for sorrows, was drawn to the hurt of the people, and was expected to deal with them gently. Yet as dedicated and compassionate as he might have been, his role was a temporary one. He was not in a position to take away the sins and sorrows of the people permanently. The people came to the temple and his office time and time again because their sorrows were many and their sin ever before them required it.

But God had a plan. One would come to fulfill the role of high priest forever. This Great High Priest would be drawn to and sympathize with our weakness because he, too, would be tempted in every way. Yet amazingly enough, he would not need to make a sacrifice for his own sins because he would be sinless. He would once and for all save the people from their sins (Hebrews 4:15). The Hebrew readers sitting on the other side of the fulfillment of the promise knew this well. They just needed a solid reminder their rescuer had already come.

Why Jesus Is Better—Your True Rescuer

The man appointed high priest was a beautiful provision, but it was never meant to be permanent. God always had a plan to fill the role himself. Author and pastor Warren Wiersbe said,

> The law was holy and good, but it was limited by the frailties of the flesh. Aaron died; his sons after him also died. The priesthood was as good as the man, and the man did not last forever. But Christ lives to die no more. He has the unchanging priesthood because He lives by the power of an endless life.[4]

Holy and good as it was, the law was limited. The priesthood was as good as the man. Now, wouldn't common sense say we should want the best "man" for the job? The writer of Hebrews certainly thinks so, and he goes on to say,

> In the same way, the Anointed One, *our Liberating King,* didn't call Himself but was appointed to His priestly office by God, who said to Him,
>
> > You are My Son.
> > Today I have become Your Father,
>
> and who also says elsewhere,
>
> > You are a priest forever—
> > in the *honored* order of Melchizedek
> > (Hebrews 5:5-6 THE VOICE).

Is his audience convinced yet? He is about to make the case that Jesus is once and for all their permanent high priest forever—the only one they would need. Yet he pauses to discuss the one remaining issue keeping his readers from moving forward with fueled faith instead of backward toward legalism. They lacked spiritual maturity. He spends the end of chapter 5 and the entirety of chapter 6 drawing them toward maturity. I love that in the midst of reminding them of what they already knew (the office of the high priest) he takes time to firm up the foundation. Although he warned them sternly, he affirmed that he believed better things for them. "But listen, my friends—we don't mean to discourage you completely with such talk. We are convinced that you are made for better things, the things of salvation" (Hebrews 6:9 THE VOICE). He was ensured they were listening and ready for this conversation weighted heavy with truth. They were made for better things.

> This is no small invitation. You were made for the true rescuer. His name is Jesus, and he is so much better.

May I take a cue from the writer of Hebrews and remind you of the same? If we were still sitting at the café chatting, this might be the point where you would excuse yourself to use the ladies' room. Or maybe you would lean in and want to hear the rest. You might still be feeling a little rough from our first discussion on maturity a couple of chapters back. Maybe you're longing to make the study of God's Word your top priority, but you are weary and worn through. Perhaps you think you just can't take more of anything. Oh, sweet friend, this discussion on maturity and responsibility is not meant to push you down but to lift you up. We could pause here and shift the conversation to lighter fare, but I want you to know that, in the depths of your heart, "You are made for better things."

This is no small invitation. You were made for the true rescuer. His name is Jesus, and he is so much better.

Name Dropping, but Not Really

In the process of presenting Jesus as superior to the high priest still serving in the temple at the time this letter was written, the writer makes a comparison to someone named Melchizedek. This may seem random to us and even as though the author is offering a name drop of sorts. But the Hebrews would have instantly known who Melchizedek was and how to pronounce his name. They might have looked around at one another and said, "Oh, Melchizedek. I love that guy." So maybe in that regard it was a slight name drop. But this one had

purpose beyond getting their attention. Melchizedek was part of the
master plan of the ages. Who was he? What do we need to know about
him and about how Jesus being tied to him would help move the readers forward?

Melchizedek is mentioned in the Bible only twice, other than in
the book of Hebrews. If you turn back to Genesis chapter 14, you will
read the account of Abraham's encounter with him (which is restated
in Hebrews chapter 7):

> Melchizedek king of Salem brought out bread and wine.
> (He was priest of God Most High.) And he blessed him
> and said,
>
> > "Blessed be Abram by God Most High,
> >   Possessor of heaven and earth;
> >   and blessed be God Most High,
> >   who has delivered your enemies into your hand!"
>
> And Abram gave him a tenth of everything
>   (Genesis 14:18-20).

Melchizedek means "king of righteousness" and Salem means
"peace." Abraham met him as he was returning from defeating King
Chedorlaomer. Melchizedek, although a king, brought bread, wine,
and a blessing to battle-weary Abraham. Grateful, Abraham honored
him not only as king but as a priest by giving him a tenth of everything he had.

Hebrews 7:3 further explains, saying of Melchizedek, "He is without father or mother or genealogy, having neither beginning of days
nor end of life, but resembling the Son of God he continues a priest forever." In this description, he is considered a foreshadowing of Christ—
one who appears before the earthly life of Christ and points us to
him. Matthew Henry said, "The most general opinion is that he was
a Canaanite king, who reigned in Salem, and kept up religion and the
worship of the true God; that he was raised to be a type of Christ, and
was honored by Abraham as such."[5]

The only other Old Testament mention of Melchizedek is in Psalm 110:4, which says,

> "The Lord has sworn
>   and will not change his mind,
> "You are a priest forever
>   after the order of Melchizedek."

In this psalm David is describing his Lord. He is one forever after the order of Melchizedek—a king and priest simultaneously and forever. *This is Jesus.* In his priesthood he most resembles Melchizedek, a priest through the oath of God not by his association with the tribe of Levi, without human lineage, reigning with peace and righteousness forever.

In Hebrews the writer brings it all together by saying,

> For on the one hand, a former commandment is set aside because of its weakness and uselessness (for the law made nothing perfect); but on the other hand, a better hope is introduced, through which we draw near to God.
>
> And it was not without an oath. For those who formerly became priests were made such without an oath, but this one was made a priest with an oath by the one who said to him:
>
> > "The Lord has sworn
> >   and will not change his mind,
> > 'You are a priest forever.'"
>
> This makes Jesus the guarantor of a better covenant (Hebrews 7:18-22).

The law made nothing perfect. It was never meant to be permanent. The Levitical priests the people interacted with daily in the temple held office because of their human lineage; they served at God's Altar without an oath. They were required to make atonement for their own sins before they served the people. They were, in essence, imperfect men made priests by law. A. W. Tozer said,

> But the breakdown in the Old Testament was that the priest, when he went before God, to stand between a holy God and fallen man, was embarrassed, because he had to atone not only for the sins of the people he was reconciling, but he had to atone for his own sins as well...The priest could not, by the blood of sacrifice he made, take the sin away completely but partly.[6]

But Jesus is a priest by the oath of God. He is a better hope and became the "guarantee of a new and better covenant" (7:22 THE VOICE). He has no need of a successor because he holds his priesthood forever. Tozer goes on to say,

> When Christ came, He qualified completely as the one who could reconcile God and man. He was ordained of God. That was qualification number one. "Thou art my son. Thou are a priest forever." He wanted reconciliation for the people. He had compassion. Christ qualified as the priest, and He became the author, the source and giver of eternal salvation.[7]

Jesus, thus established as a priest forever, did not rely on the blood of bulls and goats to reconcile the people to God. He marched a pathway straight into the throne room by way of the cross.

> It is only fitting that we should have a High Priest who is devoted to God, blameless, pure, compassionate toward but separate from sinners, and exalted by God to the highest place of honor. Unlike other high priests, He does not first need to make atonement every day for His own sins, and only then for His people's, because He already made atonement, reconciling us with God once and forever when He offered Himself as a sacrifice (Hebrews 7:26-27 THE VOICE).

> Devoted to God, blameless and compassionate Jesus put
> himself on the Altar—he himself was the sacrifice.

Devoted to God, blameless and compassionate Jesus put himself on the Altar—he himself was the sacrifice. And God, being fully satisfied with the sacrifice, raised him from the dead and lifted him to the highest place of honor, where he sits at God's right hand for all of eternity. Glory.

Do you think this was a lightbulb moment for the Hebrews? Is it for you? "God became man in order to rescue sinful man. This He did by forfeiting His own life that He might bring back to God again those who had revolted. This, Jesus Christ our Lord did, and now we have Him sitting on the right hand of the throne of the Majesty in the heavens."[8] All of this, with soul-shattering detail, points to Jesus as not just a better high priest, but the best and only one they would ever need. All of this for them. To rescue us. He has settled forever their reconciliation to God and secured an unhindered lasting relationship with God for us. He sits now at God's right hand.

> The fact that He is seated is also symbolic of the posture of
> a king whose army had been victorious in battle. His not
> standing, or pacing or worrying. He has presented the perfect sacrifice for sin on our behalf, and He has obtained the
> complete victory over sin and death. He is our undefeated,
> conquering King.[9]

Your conquering king has taken a seat because the work of salvation is complete. We already talked about this in chapter 2, if you recall. What is he doing at God's right hand? Oh, girl, I'm so glad you asked.

He Prays for You

Years ago, I'm not sure it ever occurred to me what Jesus was doing in heaven. I mean, I knew he was seated; I understood that. But surely he was simply enjoying the everlasting worship in heaven—much deserved, I should say. But now that I know this truth, Hebrews 7:25

has quickly become one of my favorite verses. And being responsible for it is no difficult task. I love to share it with others: "He is able to save to the uttermost those who draw near to God through him, since he always lives to make intercession for them."

Jesus is capable to save completely those who come to God through him. He lives and "breathes" prayers out for them all the time. The Father's ear is bent toward his voice. Can you let that truth wash over your heart today? Jesus prays for you. Constantly. Have mercy, that is what our Great High Priest is doing for us today. He is talking to the Father about me. He is mentioning you by name.

But honestly, this should not surprise us at all, because in chapter 5 we read, "In the days of his flesh, Jesus offered up prayers and supplications, with loud cries and tears, to him who was able to save him from death, and he was heard because of his reverence" (5:7). When Jesus walked this earth he was already praying as your Great High Priest. He was crying out and weeping in great sorrow over what was to come, but ultimately for God's will to be accomplished. Luke tells us in his Gospel account, "Jesus repeatedly left the crowds, though, stealing away into the wilderness to pray" (Luke 5:16 THE VOICE). His life has always been about prayer, and he often slipped away to talk to his Father.

I know it may be hard for you to imagine that Jesus prays for you. Maybe you feel pretty small and insignificant. Surely, though, you have felt the peace that comes when you *know that you know* someone is praying for you. Maybe you've been in the thick of a very hard season and you have that one group of friends you can text anytime and say, "Please pray for me. I need to know you are lifting me up." As the sweet affirmations from your prayer team come back with their heartfelt words, you sense the peace and presence of the Lord wrap you up. Peace settles in hard places when God's people call on him. I have lived it. Let me explain.

Earlier I talked about my struggle with fear, specifically concerning my daughter's illness. This started last year as my family was thrown into a maelstrom when our doctor called at midnight, telling us to rush our eight-year-old to the emergency room. She'd had bloodwork

a couple of days earlier that indicated her hemoglobin was danger-
ously low. Upon our arrival they tested her once again and found it
had plunged even further. Without answers and a long night ahead
of us waiting for doctors and tests to be ordered, we made our way
to the pediatric intensive cancer care unit of our local hospital. Three
hours earlier, I was tucked in my bed at home, dreaming about jumping on a flight to visit a group of writing friends in Dallas. My weekend
was going to be filled with food, laughter, and encouragement sorely
needed. Now I was sitting with my child in a hospital room not much
bigger than a closet—waiting.

My husband stayed as long as he could, but he left once we were
settled because we had three other children at home who needed him.
We split the team because we had to. I desperately wanted to text someone to pray. But my dearest prayer warriors were of course sleeping at
three in the morning. Slowly, as the world outside woke up and the sun
edged itself toward rising, I started texting them. One by one they went
to their knees on my sweet girl's behalf. Pretty soon that prayer chain
wrapped around the world. I wholeheartedly believe "the prayer of a
righteous person has great power as it is working" (James 5:16). I felt it
working during the early morning hours in that tiny hospital room and
as the week wore on. Don't ever doubt that "knees to the floor" means
something to the person who begs for it. It certainly does.

As much as all those prayers meant to me and sustained me, the
long minutes from three until five thirty held a far deeper sense of
gratitude. Here is where I wrestled. With no one to turn to but Jesus,
I found him profoundly faithful and deeply tender. I can tell you the
silence in a tiny hospital room that time of the morning is deafening.
All I had in that moment was the One who had promised to hold me
together. And I was holding on to him with everything I had. It wasn't
much. It was small. Gratefully, God works not because of what I bring
to the moment, but because of who he is. He was enough that night,
and he will always be enough. My Great High Priest did not turn
from me. He sat with me in my hardest, most fearful moment, and he
prayed for me. I'm sure of it.

The High Priestly Prayer (A Look Straight into His Heart)

If you turn back to John 17, you can look straight into the heart of Jesus and his prayer life. This is often called the High Priestly Prayer, and it's what Jesus prayed just before the nighttime betrayal that ultimately led to his crucifixion. What did he pray about in this prayer? He prayed for himself and he prayed for his followers. In fact, Jesus prayed this prayer just after what is known as the "upper room discourse, where Jesus was primarily concerned with preparing the Twelve for life after His departure."[10] He prayed within earshot of them so they would hear it and have joy (John 17:13). But in his last lingering moments of freedom he was also looking toward the future, seeing you and me. He said, "I am not asking solely for their benefit; this prayer is also for all the believers who will follow them and hear them speak" (17:20 THE VOICE). What exactly were his prayers for us? In talking to his Father from the depths of his heart, he asked for all believers to be...

- kept and protected (11,15).
- one (11,21-22).
- immersed in truth (17).
- with them in eternity (24).
- living in love today (23,26).

This passage has much more than I can explore in the time and space allowed here. The truth is I would love nothing more than for you to study this passage on your own. As I was sitting in the coffee shop today doing that very thing, I was brought to the point of tears because I can't help but read this passage and think, *This is the unveiling of the heart of your rescuer.* Just listen.

> I will no longer be physically present in this world, but they will remain in this world. As I return to be with You, holy Father, remain with them through Your name, the name You have given Me. May they be one even as We are one. While I was physically present with them, I protected them through Your name. I watched over them closely; and only

one was lost, the one the Scriptures said was the son of destruction. Now I am returning to You. I am speaking this prayer here in the created cosmos alongside friends and foes so that in hearing it they might be consumed with joy. I have given them Your word; and the world has despised them because they are not products of the world, in the same way that I am not a product of the corrupt world order. Do not take them out of this world; protect them from the evil one...

Father, I long for the time when those You have given Me can join Me in My place so they may witness My glory, which comes from You. You have loved Me before the foundations of the cosmos were laid. Father, You are just; though this corrupt world order does not know You, I do. These followers know that You have sent Me. I have told them about Your nature; and I will continue to speak of Your name in order that Your love, which was poured out on Me, will be in them. And I will also be in them. (John 17:11-15,24-26 THE VOICE)

In his words we can hear his tenderness, sense his ache for us, and witness how he reaches for each of us in prayer. I believe it is how Jesus is praying for you now because "Jesus the Anointed One is always the same: yesterday, today, and forever" (Hebrews 13:8 THE VOICE). I wonder how I might live differently going forward if I immersed myself in this truth. It is what he prayed for me. Oh, to let it be true in my daily life. Charles Spurgeon said,

But oh, you must have Him. You must have Him. You cannot get to God without Him! I pray that you will feel such confidence in His tenderness that you may come and take Him as your own High Priest. If you do, He will be yours at the moment of acceptance. He will never refuse the seeker. He will not hide Himself from His own flesh. He will never be distant and strange to any penitent sinner. If you desire Him, it is because He desires you. And if you have a spark of wish for Him, He has a furnace of desire for you. Come, and welcome.[11]

> Jesus is your Great High Priest forever...You
> must have him. You do have him. Forever.
> He is the better you were made for.

Jesus is your Great High Priest forever. He is constantly pouring out his heart to the Father on your behalf. He will never refuse you as you seek him. He will not hide himself or be far off. You must have him. You do have him. Forever. He is the better you were made for.

And now since you know this truth, you are responsible for it. But this responsibility is not burdensome. Truly, it sets you free.

PART 2

Our Response

Unshakable

Hebrews 3:1-6; Hebrews 8:6-12; 2 Kings 17:36-41;
Matthew 16:24; 1 John 5:20-21

Summer always makes me a little bit sentimental about the way I grew up. Life was small and slow. My hometown was once called Lick Skillet, for goodness' sake. Gratefully, they changed that before I was born. We knew everyone in our community, and family was never far from your front door. In fact, our grandparents were most often found sitting in our kitchen, drinking coffee and waiting for whatever dinner my mom was going to throw together. My brother and I lived outside on hot summer nights, catching lightning bugs in jars and playing hide-and-seek with our neighbors. When my mom called us into the house we were covered in sweat and a day's worth of dirt. I assure you we slept well because we played hard.

We worked hard too. We were not farming people, but my grandpa kept a magnificent garden in our backyard. In July he would disappear among rows and rows of green beans and send bushels into the house for us to clean and can. In between, the women would gather at the table and snip them one by one for what seemed like days. We also talked and shared stories. I would sit wide-eyed as Grandma talked about dancing with Grandpa when she was young and how handsome he was in his uniform during the war. She also did not make light of the years spent raising five children at home alone while that same man, years later, drove trains back and forth between Boston and Cincinnati.

My small and quiet life had been birthed from years of hard living. I was grateful. Legacy is beautiful when generations lean over kitchen tables and keep the conversation honest and true. Mind you, it wasn't all pretty, but it was still beautiful.

The Hebrew people were proud of their hard and beautiful legacy too. When they gathered around the hearth fire they talked long into the night about men like their father, Abraham, and their king, David. But at some point, as the evening wore on, they most likely ended up talking about Moses. He was kind of a big deal. In fact, he was such a big deal the writer of Hebrews felt as though he needed to bring him up pretty quickly in chapter 3. He wanted his readers to know they were not only hung up on Moses's greatness; they were on the verge of missing the truth staring them right in the eyes.

> Therefore, holy brothers, you who share in a heavenly call-
> ing, consider Jesus, the apostle and high priest of our con-
> fession, who was faithful to him who appointed him, just
> as Moses also was faithful in all God's house. For Jesus has
> been counted worthy of more glory than Moses—as much
> more glory as the builder of a house has more honor than
> the house itself (Hebrews 3:1-3).

Surely the glimpse of Jesus worthy of heavenly worship in chapter 1 would have caught their attention. Recognizing Jesus as their fearless founder of salvation must have pricked their hearts in chapter 2. Did the writer really need to say, "Take a good hard look at Jesus. He's the centerpiece of everything we believe, faithful in everything God gave him to do" (3:1-2 MSG)? And also tell them Jesus was worth more glory than Moses? I guess he did. Sometimes we have to state the obvious.

This reminds me of the warning label my husband and I found on a baby toy we purchased for our third daughter. It was this amazing little invention called an Exersaucer. Basically, it's a plastic circle with a seat in the middle of it. The inner seat "spins" and moves, allowing the little cherub to stay upright, play, and have different views of the room. There is no way a baby can get out on her own. In fact, it's pretty hard for her parent to dislodge her chubby legs out of the seat while wiggling her back and forth. Still, this invention saved me many days as a busy mom of three. It also probably protected my little one from the excessive attention she received from her two older sisters. She was safe and secure, and my hands were free for a few minutes.

On the side of this wonderful piece of baby machinery, a warning to parents stated, "This device is not to be used as a pool floatation device. Do not use as sled." I would have assumed this to be obvious for parents. Did the manufacturer really need to tell parents the Exersaucer did not float? Or, "Hey, by the way, a baby can't go sled riding down a snow-covered hill in this. Nope. That is not a good idea." We laughed so hard at this warning, imagining our sweet Caroline speeding by all the other kids on their antiquated red wooden Radio Flyers. Of course, it was obvious to us. But as sure as I'm sitting here, some parent somewhere must have thought, *Hey, why don't we try floating this baby?* Just know, we did not. We did, however, remind her sisters several times not to try that.

I think the writer of Hebrews knew he had to speak plainly when he said not to consider Moses, but to "consider Jesus." Yet the legacy of Moses was so lodged in the Hebrews' hearts that nothing or no one could easily replace it. As faithful as Moses was, Jesus was better in every way.

> For the first-century Jewish-Christian audience, Moses is the rescuer of Hebrew slaves out of bondage in Egypt—the receiver of God's law and the covenant. They remember how he shepherded the children of Israel safely through the desert for 40 years and led them to the brink of the promised land. He was indeed a remarkable man.[1]

Moses was a remarkable servant of God. There is no arguing this point.

- Moses was called by God (3:2).

- Moses was faithful (3:2).

- Moses "brought words from God" (3:2 THE VOICE).

- "Moses brought healing and redemption to his people" (3:5 THE VOICE).

- Moses was "a witness to the things that would be spoken later" (3:5 THE VOICE).

I love that verse 5 reminds us Moses's work as a faithful servant was to serve as a foreshadowing of what was to come—Jesus. Every bit of his mission was to point to Jesus, who was better in every way.

- Jesus is the apostle and high priest of our confession (3:1).

- Jesus was faithful to God (3:2).

- Jesus was counted worthy of more glory than Moses "as much more glory as the builder has more honor than the house itself" (3:3).

- "Jesus the Anointed was faithful as a Son of that house" (3:6 THE VOICE).

Yet what Jesus accomplished for everyone—not just the Jews—is on a totally different level. Moses was indeed faithful to God and accomplished a great deal as God's servant. Jesus, too, is faithful to God, but He has accomplished what Moses could not because He is God's very own Son.[2]

If the Hebrews were going to move forward unshakable in their faith, they needed to consider Jesus, who was faithful over God's entire house. Moses was part of that house as a servant, but Jesus was faithful as a Son. Jesus was on a totally different level than Moses was. It wasn't even close. But for the Hebrew believers, their consideration of Christ was obstructed by their infatuation with a servant named Moses.

Instead of pointing them to Christ, he had become a stumbling block to them.

Of course Jesus is better than Moses, you might be thinking. That's a no-brainer, right? But before we get too critical of what seems obvious to us (proclaiming we would never float the baby in the pool with the Exersaucer), let's take a good look at our own hearts. We have stumbling blocks that trip us up, too, and at times those stumbling blocks don't just trip us up; they grow into full-blown idols. What is an idol? Anything that keeps us from Jesus. The Hebrew people knew all about idols, and so did the writer. We should, if we are going to be unshakable in our faith, too, take a page from their history books and hold fast to the solution he is placing before them.

Dancing with Idols

I sometimes think the story of God and his people reminds me of a grand dance. He chose them, rescued them, wooed them, and took them by the hand, leading them to his promised provision. His desire was for this dance to continue for all eternity. But his "partner" had a wandering eye. Time and time again he extended his hand to her. She would take it only to let go to spin around the dance floor with less worthy suitors. She rarely, if ever, heeded her true love's warning. Listen to his impassioned plea to draw her back to her rightful place.

> I am your God! Do not fear, bow down to, serve, or sacrifice to any other gods except for Me. You should only fear, bow down to, and sacrifice to Me who led you out of Egypt with My great power and an outstretched arm. Be careful to observe all the laws, statutes, ordinances, and commands I have inscribed for you. And do not revere any other gods. Remember the sacred covenant you have entered into with Me, and do not revere any other gods except Me. I am your God—your only God! You should only fear the Eternal One your God. I will deliver you from the grip of your enemies (2 Kings 17:35-39 THE VOICE).

"Beloved," he was saying, "I am your one and only. Do not chase after other gods. You have nothing to fear when you are with me. I delivered you. I will again and again." He went on to say, "Remember, I have made a sacred promise to you. I will keep my end of it, but will you? Choose me, Beloved. Do what I say, trust me always, and you will have nothing to fear."

But his Beloved did not stay constant. Instead she constantly went astray. Scripture tells us,

> But they did not listen to the Lord's message. Instead they did just as they had done when they lived in their own nations. They feared the Eternal One while at the same time serving their own idols. Their descendants have done the same ever since (2 Kings 17:40-41 THE VOICE).

God's Beloved didn't pay attention. She just kept doing the things she had always done, just as her ancestors before her. She tried to worship God, but at the same time she was also courting and loving idols. "Their children did likewise, and their children's children—as their fathers did, so they do to this day" (verse 41). Heartbreak upon heartbreak was the result for generation after generation.

> Jesus always leads us away from lesser things with the promise that he is enough. There simply isn't room in our hearts for more than him.

Lest we think this was merely an Old Testament love triangle, Jesus made mention of the same theme to his disciples when he said, "If you want to follow Me, you must deny yourself the things you think you want. You must pick up your cross and follow Me. The person who wants to save his life must lose it, and she who loses her life for Me will find it" (Matthew 16:24-25 THE VOICE). Can you hear the same heartfelt plea from the Lord? "Do you want to follow me? You must let me be the one leading you. I will lead you away from the things you think you want that will not satisfy your longing. It won't be easy. You will most likely suffer along the way. But in losing what you cannot keep, you will gain so much more. You will gain your real life—forever." Jesus always leads us away from lesser things with the promise that he is enough. There simply isn't room in our hearts for more than him.

My Heart—Christ's Home

In college I was introduced to a tiny book called *My Heart—Christ's Home*, in which the author, Robert Boyd Munger, said, "Without question one of the most remarkable Christian doctrines is that Jesus Christ himself through the Holy Spirit will actually enter a heart, settle down and be at home there. Christ will live in any human heart that welcomes him."[3] This was what the Hebrew readers were experiencing for the first time. They were living in the dawn of this remarkable Christian doctrine and finding it hard to believe that Jesus Christ himself had moved into their hearts and was longing for them to let him be at home there. Amazingly enough, this was foretold by the prophet Jeremiah and they were reminded of it by the author of Hebrews because it mattered that much. He quoted the prophet saying,

> For if that first covenant had been faultless, there would have been no occasion to look for a second.
>
> For he finds fault with them when he says:
>
>> Behold, the days are coming, declares the Lord,
>>   when I will establish a new covenant with
>>   the house of Israel
>>   and with the house of Judah,
>> not like the covenant that I made with their fathers
>>   on the day when I took them by the hand
>>   to bring them out of the land of Egypt.
>> For they did not continue in my covenant,
>>   and so I showed no concern for them,
>>   declares the Lord.
>> For this is the covenant that I will make with the
>> house of Israel
>>   after those days, declares the Lord:

I will put my laws into their minds,
   and write them on their hearts,
and I will be their God,
   and they shall be my people.
And they shall not teach, each one his neighbor
   and each one his brother, saying,
     "Know the Lord,"
for they shall all know me,
   from the least of them to the greatest.
For I will be merciful toward their iniquities,
   and I will remember their sins no more (Hebrews
     8:7-12, emphasis mine).

Jesus was the fulfillment of this prophetic promise from God through Jeremiah. While the new covenant had come, the Hebrews still had the old covenant, ushered in by Moses, ringing in their ears. What they were being offered was so much better. The old covenant was "limited in its application. By the second covenant God will deal with the hearts of men and women and they will know him and the ultimate mercy of God."[4] This new covenant mediated by Christ was marked with intimacy, inward change, and the mercy of *I Will.*

- I will put my laws in their minds.

- I will write them on their hearts.

- I will be their God (they will be my people and they will know me).

- I will be merciful to their unrighteousness.

- I will remember their lawless deeds no more.

To make sure they understood, the writer added, "With the words 'a new covenant,' God made the first covenant old, and what is old and no longer effective will soon fade away completely" (Hebrews 8:13 THE VOICE). As Matthew Henry explained, the old covenant was "antiquated, canceled, out of date, and no more use in Gospel times as candles are when the sun has risen." Likewise the new covenant was "without fault, well ordered in all things. It requires nothing but what it promises grace to perform."[5]

The Hebrews had a choice to make. They could hold on to a canceled covenant, or let grace perform what the new covenant promised. Initiated, delivered, executed, and guaranteed by Jesus, who was faithful as a Son over God's house. We have that choice as well: to let grace perform the promise in our hearts. If I'm entirely honest, I have to admit I choose flickering flames over the rising sun on many days. As I was thinking about this passage, the Lord whispered to my heart that maybe I might be holding on to some idols in my heart as well. The truth is, "You can make an idol out of anything or anyone in life. Often it's the good things that slither up unnoticed, and soon you discover that they have first place in your heart. It's high time they be dethroned."[6] Lately I've been feeling a bit battered and bruised by life and found myself polishing up some old idols that have slithered up to first place in my heart and need to be dethroned. They look like...

> fear
> weariness
> good works
> approval
> self-righteousness

Henry Blackaby said,

> Christ's death on the cross removed every obstacle that has separated—and could ever separate—people from God. Our Most Holy God is now accessible to everyone through Jesus Christ. It is we ourselves who erect any barriers that exist between God and us. What barriers are you choosing to let stand? Jesus died to bring them down.[7]

> What are you still holding on to that Christ's
> death on the cross already destroyed?

Why do I struggle with idols in my own life? I think it's because in this place my flesh must release its own will to the unseen hand of the Father. Jesus called it "denying" myself. It isn't easy, remember? May I lean in quietly and whisper these words for you as well? What are you still holding on to that Christ's death on the cross already destroyed? God wants full access to our hearts. Every idol hiding there blocks that access. Do you need to clean house and bring down some barriers too? I have a good idea the book of Hebrews has the answer.

How to Dethrone an Idol

If we want to dethrone an idol we need to give God first place in our hearts. The best way to do that is to take the advice of the writer of Hebrews and consider Jesus. What does it mean to consider Christ? The word for consider is "from the root of the Latin word for Star [and] originally means to contemplate the stars. It suggests the idea of the astronomer, and the quiet, patient, persevering concentrated gaze with which he seeks to discover all that can be possibly known of the stars which the object of his study are."[8] When was the last time you quietly, patiently, and with a determined concentration tried to discover all you could possibly know about Jesus? Take a look at what we learn in only a few verses from the book of Hebrews.

- Consider Jesus—he is God (1:3-4).
- Consider Jesus—he is made like us (2:14-18).
- Consider Jesus—he is our Great High Priest (4:15-16).
- Consider Jesus—he is an anchor in the storm (6:19-20).
- Consider Jesus—he is a mediator of a covenant of grace (8:6-7).
- Consider Jesus—he is a spotless sacrifice for our sins (9:11-14).

With Christ's death on the cross removing every obstacle for knowing him and our minds intent on discovering who he is, we will surely find him. We will be drawn to be like him as well. I love this confirmation from the apostle John:

> We know that the Son of God has come and has given us understanding, so that we may know him who is true; and we are in him who is true, in his Son Jesus Christ. He is the true God and eternal life. Little children, keep yourselves from idols (1 John 5:20-21).

Jesus came to show us what God is like. He desires to give us understanding so we can truly know him. Do you know an idol is by nature a fake? It may hold the "likeness" of what you think you want, but it will never satisfy. I love how the Message translates these verses from above: "This Jesus is both True God and Real Life. Dear children, be on guard against all clever facsimiles." The amazing truth is you have everything you need for life and godliness. Author Kevin DeYoung said, "Our desire, delight, and dependence on the words of Scripture do not grow inversely to our desire, delight, and dependence on Jesus Christ. The two must always rise together."[9] Our passion for God's Word and our love for Jesus rise and fall together.

To prove Pastor DeYoung's point, think back to the last time the busyness of life crowded out your daily time with the Lord. Did you love him more or less? Did your own self-sufficiency take root and crowd out your dependence on God? Here are a few more questions to answer:

- Do I know Jesus *more* today than yesterday?
- Is my love growing for him?
- How is my obedience to his Word?
- Do I rely on him more and more?
- In my own life, what is Jesus better than and worth more glory than?
- What am I tempted to run back to during times of trial?
- What am I considering more than Jesus when life gets hard?

We can't find the true God and real life
in a copy. Only Jesus satisfies.

Oh, sweet friend, don't rush through these questions. I believe with all my heart that "our one need is to know Jesus better, and the one clue for all our feebleness is to look to Him on the throne of heaven and really claim the heavenly life He waits to impart."[10] We can't find the true God and real life in a copy. Only Jesus satisfies. Consider him now. His endearing love is steadfast, faithful, full of justice and mercy. His love is pursuing. It never gives up on us. No matter what we want more, Jesus wants to love us and fill that space. My prayer for you is that you will have a greater love and affection for him through your encounter with the book of Hebrews. I can't think of a better gift.

A Gentle Word of Warning

Girlfriend to girlfriend, I feel as though I should deliver this next bit of news with a bag of M&M's. The dark chocolate ones are my favorite. I would even throw in a bowl of popcorn because the combination of sweet and salty is divine. Just imagine you and me sitting cross-legged from each other, diving into our individual bowls of goodness and me adding this word of warning. If you are finally at the point of saying, "Enough. I will be a woman who is unshakable. I will walk forward in my faith and declare 'Jesus is worth being first place in my life,'" your enemy will get busy too. You see, your enemy has a name, Satan, and the idols that vie for your heart are some of his best weapons against you. He does not want you to move forward in your faith. He will be happy if you quit. It would be wise of me to tell you three things I've learned the hard way.

1. Idols are not always obvious to us.

Just like we laughed about floating the baby in the pool with the Exersaucer and talked about Moses getting more glory than Jesus, the idols that want first place in your life might not be completely obvious to you. They might be good things. Years ago I had no idea one idol I was especially fond of was an idol. I prided myself (this should have been the first clue) in being self-sufficient. I don't really need a lot of help to get things accomplished. I'm pretty smart in a bookish kind of way. I work hard. I'm capable and dependable. People love that about me, and because of that I assumed being self-sufficient was an excellent quality. The truth is it can be, but it can also keep me from my true source of strength in the Lord. When I do things by my own sufficiency, I will eventually come to the end of myself. Just know, at some point I needed someone to gently tell me my own strength taken to the extreme was nothing more than a pretty idol sitting on the shelf of my heart.

If you aren't sure what idols may be lurking around your heart, ask a friend who is willing to be a mix of grace and truth. And be ready to hear what she says and let God do the work of removing it. Just to keep you from tossing this book across the room right now, you should know that in the next chapter I'm going to tell you the whole story about how very deep my struggle has been. I'm willing to go first. And oh yes, we can go there together. That is what girlfriends do.

2. Idols don't go away willingly.

Have you ever had houseguests overstay their welcome? We all know three days is a good guideline when friends and family come to stay (except if my mom is reading this—she is welcome to stay for weeks on end because she washes the dishes and makes me breakfast). Idols don't take too kindly to being asked to leave. They linger longer than they should. In fact, they tend to band together with other idols in your life and do their best to bully you until you cave and find it easier to let them stick around.

Are you fearful? Worry will hang out there too. Is weariness pushing you down like a heavy cloak? Anger is not far behind. Are you like me and self-sufficient? Your idol BFF is named pride. Remember, they are clever and what they want more than anything is to have first place in your heart. But they will also settle for second and third place. The more the merrier.

I should probably go ahead and mention I have dethroned the same idol over and over again. It reminds me of that crazy game at the arcade called Whac-A-Mole. It seems as though no matter how many times I hit those crazy moles, they just pop right back up. The Enemy of our souls knows what has worked in our lives before. It is easy for us (and by us, I mostly mean me) to fall back into old patterns. If an idol has tripped you up before, it won't go willingly and it will probably boomerang back into your life during a time of trial. In fact, you can count on it.

3. Your enemy doesn't want you to consider Jesus.

Satan absolutely does not want you to consider Jesus. He has no time for any of that kind of contemplation. Considering Jesus will completely mess up the Enemy's plans for you. So he will do his level best to keep you so busy you won't have time. When you aren't busy, he will distract you by all the things that feel urgent and important. He will fan the flame of your fear of missing out and make you feel silly for carving out time to be with Jesus. He will probably tell you not to bother.

> You don't need Jesus and anything else, not even coffee... Jesus is truly all you need.

But if you find a tiny bit of resolve and begin to fix your eyes on Jesus with intentionality, your enemy will not just slink away quietly. He will take another approach by subtly saying, "Okay, consider Jesus. But you need this other thing too. Get you some Jesus, but hold on for dear life to your pride, your weariness, your fear." It worked for the Israelites, remember? Don't fall for it, friend. It might be the craftiest lie of all. My pastor said recently, "Jesus + Nothing = Everything." You don't need Jesus and anything else, not even coffee. And you know how I love coffee. Jesus is truly all you need.

At this point, I would probably just reach over and hand you the entire bag of M&M's and let you have at it if you were here in my living room with me. I know you don't need them plus Jesus, but we have now turned the corner and made this conversation deeply personal.

Suddenly the Hebrews infatuation with Moses doesn't seem like such a big deal, now does it? Are you feeling in any way discouraged or defeated right now? I am. And if I'm truly being honest, I have to admit I'm pretty nervous to move into the next chapter. As we turn the page together, I hope you will see my heart is open and ready to walk into an idol God is asking me to dethrone yet again. The roots go deep, and it is high time I start digging.

Maybe your struggle is similar. Or perhaps the idol that sparkles the brightest on your shelf is something different. It really doesn't matter what it's called; the solution is the same for both of us. My need and your need is to know him better. Period. So let's do what girlfriends do best. Let's hold each other up in prayer and walk together.

Oh, and pass me the M&M's.

The Cease to Do

Hebrews 3:7–4:11; Psalm 95:8-11; Colossians 3:16-17

He said it of course with a wink and a smile.

"It's a good thing you look like your mom. She's a whole lot prettier than me," my dad would knowingly tease, usually when my mom was standing within hearing distance. This way he killed two birds with one stone. My response was usually to nod in agreement. After all, my mom is a beautiful woman. It never bothered me one bit when she worked at my high school that people often got us confused. I do look a lot like her.

The older I get, and I think especially since my dad passed away, the more I realize I may look a lot like my mom, but my personality is more like my dad's.

Responsible.

Relater.

Communicator.

Like father like daughter, you might say. Mostly, that is a good thing. These qualities are certainly strengths my father handed down to me. They serve me well as I move forward, keeping order and doing all the things by the book. My dad, of course, knew this about me and perhaps saw his own ways reflected in my performance. I remember a conversation we had one time during my college years when I was a bit frazzled and busy from the pull of my own strengths. In the midst of feeling as though I couldn't do one more thing, someone had asked me to do just that. I was probably complaining to him when he repeated something he was fond of reminding me: "Do you know what to do if you need something done and you can't do it? Give it to a *busy* person. They will always get it done." I smiled, knowing he was right.

I was juggling so many things at this point in my life. But, hey, what was one more thing to toss into the air? I was bad at telling others no and at the same time good at making sure nothing dropped or was left undone. Except for the fact that deep within my heart I was fast on the way to becoming undone. I was on a collision course with myself and I was my own worst enemy. The undoing would come over and over again. I rarely learn my lessons the first time. Unfortunately, it would take years before I realized sometimes good things become bad things when we let them take first place in our lives.

Remember our conversation about idols in the last chapter? This one has my name all over it. Some people call it being a people pleaser; others might say I'm a good girl. I would probably say yes to both. I have also come to see that my desire to be self-sufficient has driven me beyond exhaustion for weeks on end. It doesn't help that I care deeply what you and others think of me. Don't get me wrong. I love Jesus with all my heart, but sometimes the voices that push me sound more like mine and yours than his. In fact, I have willingly become a slave to them.

The people of God's heart, Israel, were slaves too. They knew all about keeping and doing in the land of Egypt. In fact, they were so good at it, even when God took them to the edge of the promise they could not step into the rest he was inviting them to partake. Do you know what a busy keeper and doer has no ears to hear? *Be still. Rest. Stop doing.* You might as well throw a bucket of ice water on us in the middle of a sweltering day and watch the steam rise up for entertainment. Typically, telling us to rest has no effect. Rest is freedom's sweet song, but slaves do as slaves have always done.

The people of God had been doing the opposite of rest their whole lives. They had to work for every one of their basic needs from the beginning. When they walked out of physical bondage across the dry riverbed and through the desert, they carried everything they owned—in essence, more work. God's promise of rest must have been foreign to their ears. They simply couldn't conceive of it. Years of doing and working gave them hard hearts when what they truly needed were changed hearts. The only way that was going to happen was for them to admit their complete dependence on the Lord. They would need by faith to accept that "we do not live by the work of our hands, but by the bread and Word that God supplies."[1]

But how do you do that when everything within you is bossing you around to do otherwise? I have my own story to tell—I'm guessing you saw that coming. But before I out myself entirely, let's look at what the writer of Hebrews said to the children of slaves who were themselves standing on the edge of the new promise, thinking they might not be able to take the step of faith needed.

Make Sure You Pay Attention to This

Once again the writer of Hebrews digs into the story vault available to him and illustrates a vital truth with real-live people. Story pulls us into the truth like nothing else. Great Bible teachers know this. Take Dr. Howard Hendricks, longtime professor at Dallas Theological Seminary, for example. He "used to challenge his students with the command 'Incarnate the truth.' To *incarnate* is to make something become flesh. Don't merely discuss the truth; make the truth become living flesh so that others might be drawn to the Author of truth."[2] This story about rest and belief is going to put powerful flesh on what the Hebrew readers needed not only to hear, but to see. They were being drawn to the Author of truth. I think it will do the same for us.

> Therefore, as the Holy Spirit says,
>
> > Today, if you hear his voice,
> > do not harden your hearts as in the rebellion,
> > on the day of testing in the wilderness,
> > where your fathers put me to the test
> > and saw my works for forty years.

> Therefore I was provoked with that generation,
> and said, "They always go astray in their heart;
>   they have not known my ways."
> As I swore in my wrath,
>   "They shall not enter my rest" (Hebrews 3:7-11).

This passage is a direct quote from Psalm 95:7-11, which in turn tells the story of God's people who heard his voice and put him to the test in the wilderness (found in Exodus 17:2-7). I love to see the thread that weaves through God's Word as we study it. I think it shows us his intentionality and the truth he so desperately wants us to know. Hebrews. Psalms. Exodus. It all connects, my sister, and this story is going to be such a great reminder that God cares about the details enough to keep reminding us. Let me see if I can incarnate this truth in a way a girlfriend would, because that is what we would do if we were cooking in our separate kitchens and trading messages on my favorite walkie-talkie app called Voxer.

A girlfriend might say to another girlfriend, "Don't you just want to say, 'Bless their ever-lovin' hearts' to the Israelites?" It's true; in smashing form they just keep getting things wrong and falling short. I feel the same way about my kids when they make the same mistake over and over again. Someday, I think, they will learn. Still, because I love them, I don't just let them slip by without warning or discipline. This story is truly the heart of a Father for his wayward children. As we dive in, please lean in and see that.

Israel saw the works of God in Egypt and how he parted the Red Sea. He liberated them and provided for their daily needs. But they had a habit of complaining because deep down they did not believe God. This led to disobedience in their lives and they did not enter the rest God had provided for them. When they arrived at a place called Rephidim, they fell back into complaining. Nasty habit that complaining is, once it has a hold on your heart it is so much easier to just keep doing it. Do you want to know why they complained this time? They were thirsty. Parched. In need of a cool drink when all around them was sand. Instead of trusting God, they blamed the first guy they could think of. That happened to be Moses and they were about to kill him over their lack of water. You know, the guy who led them out of Egypt? Yes, that guy. I think he was probably used to it. Still, God in his mercy gave them water. I love this interchange:

> Moses had had enough of their complaints, so he cried out to the Eternal One.
>
> **Moses:** What am I supposed to do with these people and their relentless complaining? They are on the verge of stoning me.
>
> **Eternal One** (to Moses)**:** Here's what I want you to do: go on ahead of the people and take some of the elders of Israel with you. Also, be sure to bring your shepherd's staff—the one with which you struck the Nile. I will be there when you arrive standing at the rock of Horeb. I want you to strike the rock with your staff; and when you do, water will flow out of it so that everyone will have enough to drink.
>
> The elders of Israel accompanied Moses and watched as he did what the Eternal directed.
>
> Moses named the place Massah and Meribah, because the Israelites complained and tested the Eternal, saying, "Is He standing with us or not?" (Exodus 17:4-7 THE VOICE).

Moses had had enough of their complaining. I think Moses broke apart because Scripture says he *cried out* to God. The Hebrew word for *cried* here is *tsa'aq*, which means "to shriek" or an "outcry."[3] Y'all, Moses was over it and he cried out loudly, "What am I supposed to do with these people?"

Still obviously sore from this event, Moses called it "Meribah," which means bitter strife (clearly) and "Massah," which means "testing" (to put it mildly). Israel watched water flow out of a rock, because the same God who parted the sea cared that they had something to drink. But he also passed judgment on them by allowing the soldiers from Amelek to come and attack them in that place. He saved them from that attack as well, because again the heart of the Father for his children is one of freedom and rest. They just had to learn the hard way. So much so, that God did not let them enter his rest at that time. Instead they walked for 38 more years in the wilderness until the older generation all died out. Warren Wiersbe called it "the world's longest funeral march," and truly it was.

The Israelites were living in who they once were instead of who God was calling them to be. They heard God's voice but they did not combine what they heard with faith. Their unbelief combined with their unfaithfulness broke God's heart. Unbelief happens when we don't hear or understand God's voice. Our hearts are stubborn or obstinate and we are led away from the truth. As a result we are faithless. This grieves the heart of God because he knows unbelief and hardness of heart go hand in hand. It certainly did for the Israelites. There is a bittersweet warning for us here. I don't want to miss it, do you?

The best news is that hearing and believing also go hand in hand. Faith softens our hearts. When God speaks, we need to take him at his word no matter how unbelievable it is. The writer of Hebrews continues:

> Take care, brothers, lest there be in any of you an evil, unbelieving heart, leading you to fall away from the living God. But exhort one another every day, as long as it is called "today," that none of you may be hardened by the deceitfulness of sin. For we have come to share in Christ, if indeed we hold our original confidence firm to the end (Hebrews 3:12-14).

The writer of Hebrews uses this story to warn these new Hebrew believers not to harden their hearts and miss what God has for each of his children. The first generation out of Egypt missed the rest of Canaan. They traded it for wilderness and wandering. He is saying, "Be careful, my friends, that today you don't become hardened by sin and miss the best of what God has for you." In the book of Hebrews, the rest the writer is referring to is the peace and salvation we have in Christ.

That rest is truly twofold: first we have the gift of salvation and future Sabbath rest in the glory of heaven. But we also have rest here and now through our relationship with Jesus. Simply put, in both cases the Israelites and the Hebrew readers aren't slaves anymore. Guess what! We aren't either. We get to rest from the keeping and the doing.

> So first of all rest means to cease from action or motion—you stop doing what you are doing. The action and the motion is over. It means to stop from labor or exertion. Now applying that to God's rest, it means no more self-effort. No more trying to please God by your feeble, fleshly works. And the moment you enter into God's rest, works cease as a way to please God. They don't please Him anyway because you can't do enough to be perfect. And so rest then involves cessation from legalistic activity. It is rest in free grace.[4]

This makes it a bit more personal, doesn't it? How are we doing with the self-effort and trying to please God and all the people with our own ridiculously long lists of fleshly works? I think perhaps it is time for me to insert a bit more of my story. Because as much as I like watching the object lesson of a million or so hardhearted wilderness wanderers, I have a more personal story to tell that might hit closer to home for you too.

So You Feel As Though You've Been Here Before

When I was a little girl, our city park had a set of swings called the Witch's Hat. They were dangerous in every way, as most items at the playground were in the 1970s. It makes me laugh a little bit now because as a mother of four there is probably no way I would have ever let my kids get on something called the Witch's Hat.

My dad played softball so we lived at the park most summers. When we arrived at the playground we would run as fast as we could to these swings. The Witch's Hat had a pole with a clown face in the middle and a cross bar with two swings on opposite sides. This was not your typical swing set. It required a partner to make the swings fly. So if you were lucky to have your big brother with you, and he was willing, you would sit in one swing and he would take the other swing and use it more like a harness around his waist. He would then grab hold of the pole with one hand and your swing with the other and start walking around the pole slowly. This action would set your swing into motion. If he did it right and you were still lucky, at just the right moment he would jump into his swing and launch you into the stratosphere.

Somebody probably complained or got hurt, because one day they removed the Witch's Hat, much to every child's dismay. The park was never the same after that.

The Witch's Hat was a fun ride, but it didn't really go anywhere. In fact, every time you went around the circle on your swing you'd get the same blurred view. After a while you just closed your eyes because there was nothing new to see. Part of my story feels a little bit like that. Some days it seems I'm going round and round in circles. It has that, "I feel like I've been here before" feeling, because I have. Other times, I feel stuck like a child sitting on one side of the Witch's Hat, waiting patiently for another child to show up to make the ride go fast and high. Lately, I've been feeling both. God has pressed hard on my heart the past few days. I have not slept. I have been distracted and avoided sitting down to tell you about this. I have even claimed to be "word dead." But I know if I want to move forward with faith, if I want to go anywhere other than where I've been, it's time to put my childish ways behind me and embrace the set-free woman God wants me to become.

Years ago, sometime after the Witch's Hat and sometime before I had children, I had a job interview that involved references from people who knew me well. The interviewer hadn't just asked them why I was awesome and should get the job; she also asked them what might be my greatest hindrance to doing the job well. Each and every personal reference said essentially the same thing:

"Stacey has a hard time saying no."

"Stacey is a people pleaser of the highest degree."

"Stacey wants people to like her. A lot."

I smiled awkwardly and said, "Yes. That sounds like me." I really didn't see why all those things were so bad. It wasn't as if I was a bad person. No, I was truly good at being good. And doggone it, I wanted people to like me. Mostly, they did.

The interviewer looked down at her paper and then to me, and said, "You know these all sound like good things, but they might cause problems for you in a job like this. If you're going to be part of our team, you'll need to work on this." I wanted to crawl under the table. A memory also flashed into the forefront of my mind from a few years earlier. A godly woman had told me, "Fear of failure dominates your life." That conversation sent me into a tailspin for weeks. Here I was going round and round that Witch's Hat. Again. Same old blurred view of life. Only this time I think I might have uttered to myself as I left the interview, "Well, I need do a better job of hiding that in the future." And so I did.

I got the job and for the most part it went pretty well. Sometime later my life shifted when we started our family and moved across country. Suddenly the people I most wanted to please weren't people like my employer; they were my kids. Sweet as they were (and still are), they didn't seem to notice I was working myself weary for their endless needs. I was fearful and careworn and unsure how to fix it or even if I wanted to.

About this time, I met a writer, Emily Freeman. She was working on a new book and asked a few women to read it and give her feedback. I am sure it wasn't a coincidence that she asked me to be one of them. People pleasers can spot each other from a mile away. Just like athletes have secret handshakes only they know and understand, other "good girls" have a sixth sense about each other. Even if you only know them from the internet. You just know. Her book is aptly called *Grace for the Good Girl*.

I eagerly read it until I got about a third of the way in and suddenly didn't like it. I wanted to stop reading, and it wasn't because it was poor writing. On the contrary, it was some of the best writing I had read recently. I emailed Emily something like this: "I'm struggling. This is hard. Is it just me?" She was kind enough to tell me my email was not the only one she had received from the group. Good girls want to know they are not alone. Apparently, I was not.

I set the book on my nightstand and tried to avoid it. I wanted to stop because it was hitting too close to home. Normally, at this point with a book, I'd put it aside and come back to it later. Maybe. But I had made a commitment. I said I'd read it. I said I'd review it. I had to finish it. Good girls do what is expected of them. May I tell you something? I'm glad I did. She understood me because we were a lot alike.

> We live and breathe and move on this terrestrial masquer-
> ade ball, longing to display the prettied up exaggerated ver-
> sion of ourselves to everyone else. Behind my pretty mask I
> was a worried, anxious wreck of a girl.[5]

My own good-girl masquerade was fashioned by responsibility and the expectations of others. I was worried about what others thought about me. My friends were right to say so. Oh, it wasn't that I sat around wondering, *Does she like me?* No, I worried that I would let others down and they would think badly of me. I wondered what I was supposed to be doing in any given moment. Sitting still and resting were nearly impossible for me. I wanted to please God. I wanted to please my family. And I wanted to please everyone else. My willingness to trust God was clouded by this desire. I was busy with so many things. Trust just wasn't one of them.

Like Israel and my friend Emily, what I was really good at was keeping and doing. I'm a doer. I do. I work hard. I like keeper and doer verses in the Bible about doing and working hard. I have a whole collection of them written on 3 x 5-inch cards. Do you want to know my life verse? It will not come as a surprise to you that it just happens to be the ultimate keeper and doer verse. I didn't plan this; it simply became my verse over the years. No other verse describes my passion for God's Word and the strength he has given me through it. My love for this verse grew from 2008 to 2010 when I spent time studying it word by word.

> Let the Word of Christ richly dwell within you, with all
> wisdom; teaching and admonishing one another with
> psalms and hymns and spiritual songs, singing with thank-
> fulness in your hearts to God (Colossians 3:16 NASB).

Can you see that the keeping and doing parts of this verse make it attractive to good-girl people pleasers like me?

I can do dwell.

I can do teach.

I can do admonish.

I can do sing.

But as I claimed this verse as my own, I missed one very small but very big and important word that sets off this entire verse.

Let.

I steamrolled over that little word. Do you know why? I couldn't do *let*. *Let* had no appeal to me. It means to inhabit. To dwell in. The reason it's at the beginning of this verse is that the "letting" is to come first. Letting the Word of Christ dwell within you first. And then everything else follows.

Ironically, or not so much, Emily Freeman wrote about "let" in her book. She said, "Therefore, come now. The dreaded words of sacrifice. The bridge between how things were and how they will be. The call to move beyond perceived control into a cautious holy trust."[6]

Honestly, this made me shake in my boots when I read it. I saw who I wanted to be. I saw who I was: a worn-out weary wisp of a girl who was on a collision course with self-destruction. And the bridge from my then-current reality to the woman I wanted to be was a tiny three-letter word called *let* filled with a whole lot of holy trust.

But guess who was standing on the other side, cheering me on? The One who is the very Word of God. The One who already dwells within me. The One to whom I had been pouring out my thanksgiving over the years largely because of this verse. Emily went on to say, and I love this part so much, "He doesn't sit at your table feeble and frail...He stands strong at the head, graciously filling your plate with all that he is. He lavishes us with a godly inheritance."[7] And truthfully, I realized he wasn't only waiting on the other side for me. He was with me. He was behind me. He was ahead of me. My letting had more to do with him than it did with me. I think somewhere along the way, as my "self" got bigger, I made him a little smaller and forgot who he was. Emily's book wrecked and righted me in the best way possible and helped me remember who God was. And for a time, the letting flowed from an honest place.

About Those Idols That Boomerang Back into Your life

I wasn't kidding in the last chapter when I said, "If an idol has tripped you up before, it won't go willingly, and it will probably boomerang back into your life during a time of trial. In fact, you can count on it." Guess what has slithered back into my life like a bad movie remake? Yes, my keeper and doer have been fighting once again for first place. As I've been studying this particular passage in Hebrews on Israel and rest, my enemy has been leaning in to whisper to me, "You are such a hypocrite. Why are you writing these words for these women? You have not arrived. You couldn't possibly have anything to say about rest because you are still a people-pleasing good girl." I'd like to say I sent him back where he belonged. But I didn't. Not right away. And that is where my struggle has come from. I was close to letting him have the upper hand when the Lord gave me a glimpse of something that has made all the difference in the world.

In Hebrews chapter 4 the writer once again warns the readers to be careful and not miss the rest God offers his people.

> That's why, as long as that promise of entering God's rest remains open to us, we should be careful that none of us seem to fall short ourselves. Those people in the wilderness heard God's good news, just as we have heard it, but the message they heard didn't do them any good since it wasn't combined with faith (Hebrews 4:1-2 THE VOICE).

It Is His Rest

First, the rest offered to us is not our own rest. It isn't akin to a Sunday afternoon nap, as holy as that may seem on truly weary days. This rest belongs to God. It is "his rest." He dwells there. The good news, the gospel truth, is that the work of our salvation is complete. You can't be accepted or loved more than you already are. "God gives us our position of rest. He brings his Son's finished work and presents it to us, and then he says, 'Please sit.'"[8] Remember back in Hebrews chapter 1 when the writer said, "After making purification for sins, he sat down at the right hand of the Majesty on high" (1:3)? Because Jesus is sitting, you can too. "'Sitting' is an attitude of rest."[9] Oh, girls, it is time to accept the rest of God and quit trying to prop ourselves up with our own works of good.

Rest Remains Open to Us

Out of his goodness and grace he still holds that promise out to us with an open hand. We haven't missed it and it doesn't have anything to do with us anyway, because the promise has its source in God. We are not beyond hope. All our keeping and doing and pretending is not needed to achieve a level where we can give ourselves permission to rest. Does that cause you to exhale a little bit? It does for me.

What is our part in it? The writer says not to fall short, which has to do with our faith. Since he was writing to believers, we need to understand that he wasn't talking about the eternal rest we have once we are daughters of Christ. We fall short when we forfeit our daily rest and unbelief creeps in. You might even let the Enemy whisper in your ear like I did this week. Our faith is a reminder we have a relationship with God that is secure. When we remember the who of rest (Christ) and the how of rest (the cross) our faith is stirred up. I said earlier when talking about Israel that faith softens our hearts to hear from God. When he speaks we need to take him at his word no matter how unbelievable it is. The Hebrews, like the Israelites, were in danger of staying fearful, not faithful. They were living in who they once were instead of who God was calling them to be. I admit sometimes I do too. But it gets even better. Really, it does.

Think about this: From the beginning of the world God's plan for us was that we would first rest.

God Prepared the Place of Rest Himself

Think about this: From the beginning of the world God's plan for us was that we would first rest. You and I don't move toward rest as his daughters; instead, God has given us the invitation to start there and move from it. The title of this chapter comes from one of my favorite little books by spiritual giant Watchman Nee. In it he says,

> Whereas God worked six days and then enjoyed Sabbath; for God works before he rests, while man must first enter into God's rest, and then alone can he work. Moreover, it was because God's work of creation was truly complete that Adam's life could begin with rest. And here is the Gospel; that God has gone one stage further and completed also the work of redemption, and that we need to do nothing whatever to merit it, but can enter by faith directly into the values of his finished work.[10]

Sabbath Rest. Canaan Rest. Daily Rest. Can you see that God is all about rest? In every instance he did the work and prepared a place where we could hide ourselves within the shelter of his wings. The same gospel has been preached throughout the ages. And in every case, the way we enter that rest is by faith.

> Sabbath Rest. Canaan Rest. Daily Rest. Can you see that God is all about rest?

I want to end this discussion with this confession and challenge. I don't want to be stuck in a place of keeping and doing. Nor do I want to spin around and around the same circle of relentlessly learning the same lesson. It doesn't matter if I call it "let" or "rest"; the source is the same and my struggle has been fierce for as long as I can remember. But what I have realized through this study of the book of Hebrews is that rest is part of my sanctification process. *Sanctification* is a big word that means I am growing in the grace of God and becoming more like Jesus every day. My pastor reminded us recently, "Becoming like Christ is like putting on clothes that don't quite fit you yet." I can cooperate in that process by putting on "those clothes" and growing in my trust in the Lord. Gradually, the clothes fit a little better every day. As I trust, I cease to do and resting in him becomes more like second nature—his, of course.

I think this is what the writer of Hebrews meant when he said to be careful and not fall short. I'd much rather cooperate than fall short, wouldn't you? Here are a few things I'm going to be focusing on as I practice moving from rest and letting God do what he wants to do in and through me:

- **Listen:** Faith comes from hearing the Word of God (Romans 10:17), and since God has spoken to us in these final days through his Son (Hebrews 1:2), I'm going to read his Word and hide it in my heart daily.

- **Position:** "I receive everything not by walking but by sitting down, not by doing but by resting in the Lord."[11] I will remember that my position starts by remembering Christ is seated, and I'm seated within him. That will be the position of my heart and I will check myself on a regular basis with the heart question, "Stacey, are you sitting today?"

- **Linger:** Part of the reason I struggle so much is that I sit with Jesus in the morning, but then I rush throughout my day and forget to let the truth I learned there linger in my heart. This is my greatest challenge. Maybe it is for you too. The growth I long for is in this area: my heart is trusting in the Word of Christ, and sitting with him in heavenly places not just at 6 a.m., but at three o'clock and 9 p.m. as well.

We received the same promises as those people in the wilderness, but the promises didn't do them a bit of good because they didn't receive the promises with faith. If we believe, though, we'll experience that state of resting. But not if we don't have faith. Remember that God said,

Exasperated, I vowed,
  "They'll never get where they're going,
    never be able to sit down and rest" (Hebrews 4:2-3 MSG).

Girlfriend to girlfriend, let's make sure the promises do us more than a bit of good. Let's hold tight to them. Let's remind each other of what we have in Christ. And for goodness' sakes, let's remind all the good girls to sit down.

Rest, my sweet sister. The promise still stands.

Faithful

Hebrews 11; Habakkuk 2:3-4; Philippians
2:6-11; Exodus 1:17–2:10

Bookstores.

Don't get me started on how much I love bookstores. I know it probably makes me seem a bit old-fashioned, but I still love walking into a brick-and-mortar store and seeing books doing their best to charm their way off the shelf into my hands. It also helps if I have a good cup of dark-roast coffee in my hand. This makes for the perfect combination of lingering in my world. Bookstores, thankfully, have caught onto this magical combination of caffeine and words. I've even heard rumors lately that the small mom- and pop-owned bookstores are making their comeback. Which reminds me, I love a comeback story best of all. Lucky for me and you and all the book lovers that we can find story at the bookstore as well.

I know as we make our way through a bookstore we all initially judge a book by its cover. But then we pull it off the shelf and open it to look inside. We want to know, or at least I do, is this book for me? Does it have something in it that will encourage my heart, make me smile, or entertain me? If I find something that sparks my attention beyond a pretty cover, I will usually tuck it under my arm and make my way to a chair in the back to read a bit before I make the commitment to buying it. Perhaps you do that too. See, I knew we were kindred hearts from the moment we met. Girlfriends know this sort of thing almost immediately.

I'm guessing, but I'm also pretty certain, that when you initially picked up this book to peek inside you knew this chapter on faith would be here. You might have fanned through the rest of the book and thought, *Hmm. That's in Hebrews? I had no idea.* But you knew about Hebrews 11. We all do. Your pastor does. Our kids do. I did too. That probably means you come to this chapter with a set of expectations.

> "Daughter, your faith is not measured on the things you do. It is measured on whom you believe in. I am enough. Find me. I am worth it, I promise."

May I tell you a secret? I have prayed over this one fiercely. I have asked God to give me fresh eyes for words I've read a million times. The stories here will hopefully stir your faith. That is why they are here. And you should also know that I prayed for you as well. I've asked God to bring you to this chapter with a hungry heart. Because when you close the cover of this book, I don't want you to hear my words echo in your soul. I want you to hear his. I want you to hear him say, "Daughter, your faith is not measured on the things you do. It is measured on whom you believe in. I am enough. Find me. I am worth it, I promise."

A Defining Faith

Remember I said earlier the letter of Hebrews starts like a sermon? But as it unfolds word by word, the writer transitions to a letter for dear friends he cares about deeply. This new sentiment emerges around chapter 10. By the time he makes it to chapter 11, I think he is passionately pleading with his readers to think over what's important that he doesn't want them to forget. He is exhorting them with truth they can't afford to miss. If he lost them somewhere in the middle, he wants to be sure they don't forget his final few words.

This reminds me quite a bit of what has been going through my heart lately about my daughter who has just started her junior year of high school. In no time at all she will be ready to step into the wide world with her heart crammed full of everything her dad and I have been doing our best to pour into her. I realized today there are still a few gaps I want to make sure I don't forget to fill up. I want to review all the truly important things she might be tired of hearing us say as well. I care so much that we are purposeful in the next couple of years, as we have tried to be over the last 16 or so. But time is short. And growing shorter. When time is slipping by quickly, you put exclamation points where commas were before. You get busy with the business of what matters. And you say things like this with great emphasis: "Now faith means putting our full confidence in the things we hope for, it means being certain of things we cannot see" (Hebrews 11:1 PHILLIPS).

"*Now*," he says. "Right *now* I'm going to tell you what faith is. I'm not going to tell you later; I'm going to tell you now. I may have mentioned faith six times before, but right now I'm going to define it for you. What is faith? It is being fully confident in what your heart is hoping for. It is certain and true and unwavering in the things you 'cannot see.'" Can you feel his passion here? Maybe, like me, you want a super-clear bookish definition of faith so you can grab your highlighter and circle it. This is for you, my word loving friend:

- **Faith:** "Conviction of the truth of anything, belief; in the NT of a conviction or belief respecting man's relationship to God and divine things, generally with the included idea of trust and holy fervor born of faith and joined with it."

- **Relating to Christ:** "A strong and welcome conviction or belief that Jesus is the Messiah, through whom we obtain eternal salvation in the kingdom of God."[1]

> Make no mistake, faith believes with fervor-filled conviction what many will say is the unbelievable. Jesus is the Messiah.

Make no mistake, faith believes with fervor-filled conviction what many will say is the unbelievable. Jesus is the Messiah. Our faith also gives us absolute assurance. Consider this:

> Faith in what God has declared gives the soul absolute assurance and firm conviction of the reality of things which the natural eye has never seen. *Yet these things are as real to the man of faith as anything that he can see, feel, taste, smell, or handle. In fact, they become even more real, for his senses might deceive him, but the Word of God he knows to be absolutely infallible* (emphasis mine).[2]

Faith says even though you can't see it or put it on Instagram, you have something better. Your faith sees the goodness of God now, but also understands "the promise is a kind of substantial down payment of the reality coming."[3] And what is coming is your triumphant Savior, who is right now making a place for you in heaven. He is your Messiah and the Word of God confirms this. You can't see him, but it is absolutely true. Did you close your eyes and say "Amen" to that last statement? That right there is your faith being sparked and affirmed. That is a good word, is it not? But let's not stop there. Let's keep going.

> Without faith it is impossible to please him. The man who approaches God must have faith in two things, first that God exists and secondly that it is worth a man's while to try to find God" (Hebrews 11:6 phillips).

"Wait a minute," you might be saying. Let's go back to the "seeing the lovely and beautiful unseen things" definition of faith. This part says I have no hope of pleasing God without faith. Hebrews is filled with hard truth, to be sure. But before you feel disqualified, I want to assure you of something you might have missed. Your faith that believes God exists and is worth finding pleases God. The writer spends the next several verses giving you real-life examples of men and women who had faith that pleased God.

Guess what! They were far from perfectly faithful. But they still pleased God. These stories, maybe like your own, are here to remind you what is possible when you say yes to those two things: *God exists* and *he is worth it.* But if that isn't enough, he goes on in the next chapter to tell you something that will put your heart at ease. Here's a hint: That kind of faith doesn't come from you. But let's put a pin in that for now and get back to it in the next chapter.

Before we move forward with the hall of faith, I want to go backward. We need to grab a couple of verses from chapter 10 because they are connected to an old friend of mine—a farmer turned prophet turned writer who was fresh out of amazing. Hebrews chapters 10 through 12 are a beautiful illustration of Habakkuk 2:3-4. In fact, the writer of Hebrews quotes it in 10:38. This perfectly communicates the heart of what we are about to dive into.

> Look at that man, bloated by self-importance—
> full of himself but soul empty.
> But the person in right standing before God
> through loyal and steady believing
> is fully alive, *really* alive (Habakkuk 2:4 MSG).

A couple of things jump out at me from Habakkuk. First, a prideful man is puffed up and soul-empty. Do you know anyone like that? Faith has an element of humility. I read this quote by Charles Spurgeon and I can't seem to get it out of my heart. He says,

> Faith is the stooping grace and nothing can make a man stoop without faith! Now, unless man does stoop, his sacrifice cannot be accepted...Now, a man who has not faith proves that he cannot stoop. He has not faith for this reason—because he is too proud to believe!

> He declares he will not yield his intellect, he will not become a child and believe meekly what God tells him to believe. He is too proud and he cannot enter heaven because the door of heaven is so low that no one can enter in by it unless they will bow their heads. There never was a man who could walk into salvation erect! We must go to Christ on our bended knees. For though He is a door big

enough for the greatest sinner to come in, He is a door so low that men must stoop if they would be saved. Therefore, it is, that faith is necessary, because a lack of faith is certain evidence of absence of humility.[4]

Faith is stooping grace. Faith bends the knee with humility. There is no room for pride or self-importance when you are a follower of Jesus Christ. After all, he himself has shown us the humble way of faith, because,

> Though he was in the form of God, [he] did not count equality with God a thing to be grasped, but emptied himself, by taking the form of a servant, being born in the likeness of men. And being found in human form, he humbled himself by becoming obedient to the point of death, even death on a cross (Philippians 2:6-8).

So many people miss Jesus because they are puffed up by the world's view of them and they've let that be their god. In the end, their souls have paid the price. Habakkuk had his fill of soul-empty people. He wrestled in his own heart, but in the end he was a living example of a faith that questions and complains but does not shrink back. He pressed forward in faith. He realized a person in right standing before God was...

loyal
steady believing
fully alive
really alive

Oh, friends, faith makes us fully alive. Don't you want to be fully alive? That is so much better than soul-empty, don't you think? Jesus was fully alive and he emptied himself so that we might live this life of faith. His death on the cross fully pleased God. "God has highly exalted him and bestowed on him the name that is above every name, so that at the name of Jesus every knee should bow, in heaven and on earth and under the earth, and every tongue confess that Jesus Christ is Lord, to the glory of God the Father" (Philippians 2:9-11). Yes, we must go to Christ on bended knee, but the beautiful truth is he stooped in grace first. He does not ask of us anything he has not already done himself.

> Faith makes it possible to look forward with hope.

Do you have more questions than answers? Are you fresh out of amazing today without a clue where God is leading? Faith makes it possible to look forward with hope. It's the foundation for anything we will ever encounter. Let's embrace faith in our God this moment, no matter what may come.

Faith Illustrated

In the past I've been guilty of looking at this hall of faith in chapter 11 and seeing what they did as "big acts of faith." I missed the fact that their faith was based in relationship. They pleased God because they sought him and had a relationship with him. God did not put these men and women in the pages of his Word because of what they did. He put them there because of what they believed. They believed God existed. They believed he was worth it. Simply said, they walked with God and learned he rewards the seeker (11:6). And the reward was even better than they imagined because his promise was true: "Behold, the Lord GOD comes with might, and his arm rules for him; behold, his reward is with him, and his recompense before him" (Isaiah 40:10). He can't help but bring his reward with him, because he, himself, is the prize.

What did their faith look like?

- Abel had an attitude of worship that offered to God an acceptable sacrifice.

- Enoch did not experience death and was carried up into heaven.

- Noah knew God meant what he said and built an ark for the saving of his household.

- Abraham answered God's call to live in the land of promise as a foreigner.

- Sarah saw the possibility of being a mother even in her old age come true.

Faith birthed out of relationship is inspiring. But what you might not know about these people is explained in the jaw-dropping words of the next few verses.

> Each one of these people of faith died not yet having in hand what was promised, but still believing. How did they do it? They saw it way off in the distance, waved their greeting, and accepted the fact that they were transients in this world. People who live this way make it plain that they are looking for their true home. If they were homesick for the old country, they could have gone back any time they wanted. But they were after a far better country than that—*heaven* country. You can see why God is so proud of them, and has a City waiting for them (Hebrews 11:13-16 MSG).

> Their faith embraced what it could not see,
> and God was not ashamed of them.

Each one of these people, Abel all the way down to Sarah, died not yet grasping the promise in their hands. Yet they still believed. Their faith looked forward to the reward coming. Could they have gone back—shrunk back? Absolutely. Instead they displayed a faith fueled by a mighty God who was preparing something far better. They saw Jesus, from a distance. They knew their Messiah was coming and they chose the hard life that faith sometimes requires. Their faith embraced what it could not see, and God was not ashamed of them.

He was proud of them.

He was not ashamed to be called their God.

Does that speak to your heart as it does mine? If you have ever known the sting of rejection because of your faith, it should. If shame knocks on the door of your heart daily and tries to convince you that you are worthless, let that last part of verse 16 be your new anthem.

God is not ashamed of his daughters.

He knows you can choose daily to go back to your old way of life. He understands you could shrink back and not move forward. He sees you, sweet friend. He is waiting with open arms. Know that when you put one foot in front of the other and you walk with him toward his promise with eyes to the eternal, he is proud of you.

Faith Grows Faith

When my oldest daughter, Emma, was a toddler, we lived in my favorite college town: Bloomington, Indiana, home of Indiana University. My friend Lisa (the same one who invited me to the Hebrews Bible study) didn't just stop at getting me into the Word. She asked me to co-lead a Bible study for a large group of college women. Every week, about 15 girls would show up at Lisa's home. She would love on them with her winsome personality and snacks. She loved on me, too, making it my favorite night of the week.

Once we gathered in her living room, each girl would open her Bible and Lisa and I would co-lead them through our time together. We studied God's Word passionately and prayed for one another. It was always late into the night when I drove home and found my husband asleep on the couch, holding little Emma. My heart was full as I replayed our conversations and tried to get ready for bed. Many of these girls had solid relationships with Christ. I loved talking to them and dreaming about the woman my daughter would become one day. I always had one question for them when I had a chance to get them alone and take them to lunch: "Tell me one thing your parents did to help you grow into the woman you are today."

Their answers were always fascinating to me. Some 15 years later, I still remember one girl saying to me, "My parents were great but they weren't perfect. They loved the Lord. But when they messed up, they apologized." Their humility was what spurred this girl to walk with Jesus, knowing she didn't have to be perfect. She just needed to walk with Jesus and realize that although sometimes you do make mistakes, you admit it and move forward. I don't know if that girl's mom and dad ever knew how much their humility meant to her, but their faithfulness laid the foundation for her to walk with God for a lifetime. That same girl loves and serves God today in the most stunning way.

I know this isn't a perfect formula, and often faith-filled parents have faithless kids and vice versa. But very often when I've found a young person with roots of faith who walks with God, their parents did something to help grow that faith.

The memory of these conversations came up recently as I was reading through Hebrews chapter 11. One verse stood out to me that hadn't grabbed my attention before. Don't you love when the Spirit of God does that? He says, "Hey, pay attention here. There is a truth I want you to observe." The verse says, "By faith Moses, when he was born, was hidden for three months by his parents, because they saw that the child was beautiful, and they were not afraid of the king's edict" (11:23). Moses has already been a major standout character in the letter to the Hebrews. But here the writer briefly brings light to the faith of his parents. Immediately I desperately wanted to ask Moses, "What did your parents do to help you grow into a man of faith?" I love that the writer mentions them, because what they did was a picture of humble faith I'm not sure many parents would have been able to make. I had to know more about them.

The Exodus backstory tells us the king of Egypt was worried about the growing population of his Hebrew slaves. He told the midwives under his employ to kill all the male Hebrew children at birth. They refused. This is what Scripture says of these fearless women: "The midwives feared God and did not do as the king of Egypt commanded them, but let the male children live" (Exodus 1:17). I love what they told the king. They said the Hebrew women were "vigorous" and gave birth on their own before they arrived. As an aside, I am fascinated by their quick wit and gumption.

Guess what! We know God rewarded them, because the next couple of verses give us their happily ever after: "God dealt well with the midwives. And the people multiplied and grew very strong. And because the midwives feared God, he gave them families" (20-21). Their faith drew the blessing of God. He dealt well with them, blessing them with families of their own. I love that God dealt well with them. What a sweet promise.

Now, greatly angered by the midwives' lack of cooperation, Pharaoh bypassed them and went straight to the people. I sense his anger mounting, don't you? "Then Pharaoh commanded all his people, 'Every son that is born to the Hebrews you shall cast into the Nile, but you shall let every daughter live'" (Exodus 1:22). He would stop at nothing to stunt the growth of a nation he required to run his kingdom. One wonders what the man was really thinking.

Under this ruthless ruler, in striking contrast we read, "A man from the house of Levi went and took as his wife a Levite woman. The woman conceived and bore a son, and when she saw that he was a fine child, she hid him for three months" (Exodus 2:1-2). Her name was Jochebed, which means "the glory of Jehovah." She is the first person in the Bible to have a name associated with God's name. We don't know if this was her given name, or if Moses, penning the history of the Exodus years later, honored his God-glorifying mother with such a name. Either way, it is beautiful and we can assume Jochebed was more concerned about the glory of God and doing his will than about her own safety. By faith, this tiny, seemingly inconsequential family lived out their relationship with God, displaying their faith in three bold moves:

By Faith They Chose to Receive Children as a Gift in Light of the Edict of the King

By the time Moses was born, Jochebed already had at least two other children. Miriam would have been around 10 years of age, and Aaron, the older brother, perhaps was at least three years old. Knowing full well their coming child could be a boy with a death sentence, the couple received him as a gift, trusting in God's perfect plan.

By Faith They Hid Their Son

Perhaps spurred on by the demonstration of the faith of the midwives or passionately responding to her own measure of faith beating in her heart, Moses's mother (along with his father) took one look at him and resolved to hide him. "*The moment she saw her baby, she was determined to fight for his life...*As the little one lay in her lap, Jochebed felt that he had been sent from God, and that He, along with her mingled faith and love, would somehow preserve the child" (emphasis mine).[5] I love this passionate description and can visualize this faithful mother steadfastly determined to fight for her son. He would need her to do so if he had any chance of survival.

In Hebrews 11:23, you may recall, we get this added commentary: "They saw that the child was beautiful, and they were not afraid of the king's edict." Moses was beautiful and they were not afraid. The Greek word used by the writer of Hebrews for "not" is descriptive even for a small word. This negative participle *ou*, when placed in front of a word, *objectively* negates a statement, "ruling it out as fact."[6] So you could paraphrase it by saying, "By faith they ruled out as fact, fear of the king's edict." Fear was not ruling Jochebed's heart—faith was.

By Faith She Made a Basket and Put Him in the Water

When he was around three months of age, Jochebed could hide the hardy babe no longer. She lovingly weaved a basket of reeds, covered it in pitch, and put him in the river. Moses was not cast in with a death sentence, but cradled in a basket of hope as a prayer to God. He was hand delivered to the daughter of the one who wanted him dead. Are you amazed by this? Only God could do that. This woman, a princess who happened to be bathing in the river, also noticed he was beautiful and took pity on him, recognizing he was a Hebrew boy. Jochebed's reward was swift when Miriam, who had been watching nearby, offered her mother—secretly his real mother—as a nurse for the child. The princess commissioned Jochebed to raise him, no doubt paying a wage protecting their entire family as well.

I wonder if that very night Jochebed drew her children close and gave her praise to Jehovah who was her glory. Undoubtedly, as she nurtured him physically over the course of the next three years, she prayed and poured out her faith as well.

> By faith, Moses, when grown, refused the privileges of the Egyptian royal house. He chose a hard life with God's people rather than an opportunistic soft life of sin with the oppressors. He valued suffering in the Messiah's camp far greater than Egyptian wealth because he was looking ahead, anticipating the payoff. By an act of faith, he turned his heel on Egypt, indifferent to the king's blind rage. He had his eye on the One no eye can see, and kept right on going. By an act of faith, he kept the Passover Feast and sprinkled Passover blood on each house so that the destroyer of the firstborn wouldn't touch them (Hebrews 11:24-28 MSG).

We have no idea how small acts of faith will influence generations or even the people around us.

He had his eye on the One no eye can see, and kept right on going. Now, where do you think he learned that lesson? Who had taught him to keep looking for an inheritance that was unperishable, unfading, and securely kept in heaven for him (1 Peter 1:4)? As Moses grew, his faith mirrored that of his biological parents. He refused the rights and privileges of his royal house and chose a hard life with God's people because he knew a better inheritance was coming. Doesn't that remind you squarely of the definition of faith we talked about earlier? Jochebed and her husband were probably long gone by the time Moses, divinely chosen by God, led his people out of bondage across the dry bed of the Red Sea, sealing their freedom. She may have had some idea, but truly Jochebed could not have imagined that her small act of faith would birth such a leader. But isn't that true for us as well? We have no idea how small acts of faith will influence generations or even the people around us. Oh, but they do.

On Inglorious Outcomes

This feels like the crescendo of the chapter, doesn't it? Moses's parents' faith begetting the undeniable faith leader of the Hebrew people. Yes. Let's raise our hands and give our shout of praise, because this is how faith should be, right? Let's keep going and mention a few more to inspire our hearts, shall we?

> And what more shall I say? For time would fail me to tell of Gideon, Barak, Samson, Jephthah, of David and Samuel and the prophets—who through faith conquered kingdoms, enforced justice, obtained promises, stopped the mouths of lions, quenched the power of fire, escaped the edge of the sword, were made strong out of weakness, became mighty in war, put foreign armies to flight. Women received back their dead by resurrection (Hebrews 11:32-35).

Each one tells a unique story and I wish I had time to dive deeper. Might I challenge you to pick one or two names to walk with for a day or so? These mentioned above, and the nameless few you could probably figure out (hello, Daniel hiding in verse 33), are worth studying further. Let their faith fuel yours.

If only we could stop here. It feels good, right? I mean, how can we not rejoice with women receiving back their dead? Oh, but we have direct orders from the Lord not to mess with his Word and leave the parts out we would rather not read. He goes on to tell us sometimes faith doesn't give us such glorious outcomes. Sometimes they get downright messy, making us uncomfortable.

> Some were tortured, refusing to accept release, so that they might rise again to a better life. Others suffered mocking and flogging, and even chains and imprisonment. They were stoned, they were sawn in two, they were killed with the sword. They went about in skins of sheep and goats, destitute, afflicted, mistreated—(Hebrews 11:35-37).

What stands out to me about these people in particular is that their lives of faith were painful and embarrassing. They were certainly mistreated. They were real people who had feelings like we do. They weren't superhuman. They were simply servants who loved God and chose faith over comfort—even life. This list should move us. It should cast our gaze beyond outcomes. We can't measure faith by what we can see. God doesn't. Walls came down by faith, but others commended by faith lived hard and difficult lives of loss, pain, and persecution. Ultimately the faithful seek a promise beyond earthly victory and reward. A promise anchored in heaven—where moth and rust cannot destroy (Matthew 6:19).

I like what my friend Katie Orr said: "Exhibiting faith does not guarantee a glorious outcome (not in our earthly terms anyway). Living a life of faith does not secure a life of comfort, riches, and good health. In fact, many modern-day heroes of faith live with constant hunger, lingering disease, and impending danger."[7]

> Sometimes exemplary lives are not rewarded on earth because God has something better planned. And his reward ultimately ends in glory.

God had an opinion on these faithful few as well. He said, "The world was not worthy of these saints" (Hebrews 11:38 THE VOICE). Sometimes exemplary lives are not rewarded on earth because God has something better planned. And his reward ultimately ends in glory.

> All these, though commended through their faith, did not receive what was promised, since God had provided something better for us, that apart from us they should not be made perfect (Hebrews 11:38-40).

It was God's plan that their faith and our faith would come together and make a complete picture. They looked forward to Christ and obtained their promise in heaven. We look back, seeing their faith, and we have received the promise because of the life, death, and resurrection of Jesus. Only he completes the picture.

Is Jesus Worth It?

I think if you could ask each one of these men and women in the hall of faith, "Is Jesus worth it?" they would all say yes. What they gave up was nothing compared to living a life of faith with their eyes set on the promise of eternity. Truly, the world was not worthy of them. May I tell you something? Because of your faith, the world is not worthy of you either, dear girl.

What a beautiful word from God. How do we find ourselves in such company? We press on by faith. Jesus is worth it. We know the full story.

The One Thing You're Really Going to Need

Hebrews 12; Romans 5:3-5; Romans 15:4

My pastor usually starts reminding us in November that January is coming and he wants us to be ready. You see, every year he asks us to pray and seek God's heart on a word to frame our upcoming year. Sometime before the last Sunday in December, he tells us his word for the year and encourages everyone in the pews to share theirs with a neighbor.

At this point I typically have word envy. Take my friend Angie, for example. Her word for this year was *freedom*. I mean, really, who doesn't want freedom in her life? I know I do. I like that word. I also like words like *victory* and *rest*. "I could sure work those words into my year, Lord," I reminded him. "Words like *victory* and *freedom* make great T-shirt slogans I can share with the world." But he had other plans for me. Plans—I have to say if I'm totally honest—I was reluctant to embrace.

Sometimes I pray and wait for weeks before the Lord brings a word to me. Not this year. I knew straightaway what the Lord was speaking to my heart. But in toddler-like fashion I was busy putting my fingers in my ears, saying, "I can't hear you, God" and singing, "Blah, blah,

blah." Mature, right? I can be. May I tell you what truly sealed the deal for me? It was Elisabeth Elliot. She was featured on a podcast marking the sixtieth anniversary of her first husband's martyrdom. Jim Elliot and four other missionaries gave their lives while serving the Auca Indians of Ecuador in 1956. Their faith (and quite frankly, hers) has inspired countless believers all over the world to serve the Lord whole-heartedly. They said, "Jesus is worth it," and it cost them everything.

Elisabeth Elliot passed away in 2015, so the podcast was a record-ing of a talk originally given at a conference held by Campus Crusade for Christ to a stadium full of college students in 1983. Yes, that's right. God used a talk from KC83 (as it was known) to bring the final word on my word for this year. Her topic was on "endurance," and this quote was what gripped my heart from the beginning. She said, "If it's God's will that you want more than anything else in the world, it's going to mean endurance."[1]

I knew it. In that moment I knew God was calling my year to be about *endurance*. I had a feeling it wasn't a great sign of what was to come. I truly wanted to choose another word. I pleaded with God. He didn't budge one inch.

Do you know what endurance means? It means "not losing heart," and by mid-January I understood. I found my theme resonating in a verse from Romans. It also happens to be the verse we talked about when we learned about Abraham. God often puts verses on repeat in my life, and this one, this year, has come up multiple times. It says, "We also celebrate in seasons of suffering because we know that when we suffer we develop endurance, which shapes our characters. When our characters are refined, we learn what it means to hope and anticipate God's goodness" (Romans 5:3-4 THE VOICE). There I was in the refin-ing process, only a couple of weeks into the year, looking with expecta-tion of his goodness. I wanted more than anything to do his will, so I asked him once again, "Lord, really? Suffering leads to endurance? Are you sure about this for me right now?"

"Endurance," he reminded me again. And then he added, "Remem-ber, 'Hope does not put us to shame, because God's love has been poured into our hearts through the Holy Spirit who has been given to us'" (Romans 5:5).

I was counting on that hope part.

By the third week of February I was a mess. It *started* with me dropping a dozen eggs on the cold tile floor of my kitchen. The rest of the week pretty much followed suit. And I must admit I felt just as broken as those eggs. I had planned on this being a tough week. My daughter was scheduled for a brutal test on Thursday that required an entire day of preparation. She fasted. So did I. By evening we were both tired, hungry, and cranky. She was facing another phase of prep that required her to drink something she was dead set against, and it wasn't going well. My husband came home and sent the other girls and me to Chick-fil-A, telling me to eat something. My fasting wasn't doing any of us any good.

When I returned, I took over the mission at hand. He hadn't made much more progress than I had. From that point on, I probably broke every parenting rule in the book. Finally, with the firmness of a drill sergeant, I set the timer on my phone and the cup was emptied minute by minute. By the time bedtime rolled around my daughter and I were both exhausted. She slept. I didn't.

The next day was a mix of more emotions than I can possibly express. How can you put into words what it feels like to follow your child into a procedure room and watch as they put her to sleep? To step away from her with a gentle kiss on the hand is like jumping into a turbulent sea. I found solace in a mediocre cup of coffee and the company of the only other person on earth who understood—my husband. And we waited.

I wrestled too. You should know, it didn't matter much that I had been in that place just the year before. Truthfully, it probably made it harder. In the few months since that first soul-breaking week with our daughter, we daily battled a mystery we couldn't quite pinpoint. Her health continued to worsen no matter what we tried. Here we were being reminded once again through this new series of tests that we might never be able to fix it. How do you look your girl in the eyes and tell her all the treatment, all the pills, all the food she has had to pass on, and all the tests have not proven helpful? She was only nine years old at the time. It breaks you. It broke me. And honestly, I just sat down and wept.

When the test was over and done with, we took her to Panera and let her eat whatever she wanted. We didn't tell her anything the doctor said to us in the waiting room until the next day. The new treatment they ordered would be another test of wills. She must have known because she started asking questions we knew we couldn't avoid anymore. I think her response was better than mine. That has been the case more times than I care to admit.

There I sat, trying to make peace with it all. I did my best not to lose heart. And I knew what I was supposed to do. I knew the truth of God's goodness, and I had his promise already tucked in my heart from Romans 5:5. I knew he was present with us. I knew he would hold us no matter what I was feeling. I knew this, because the last time I was here his faithfulness was not void. And the time before that time it was also true. But all those things being true didn't make it any easier. Do you sense a theme with endurance? Easy is not part of its vocabulary.

Over the next couple of months our family went through some of the most intense times of our lives. The longer it wore on, the more endurance I felt I needed. Like a runner in a marathon, I was longing to see the finish line that didn't seem to be anywhere in sight. What God offered me instead, in his perfect timing, was a bit of refreshment. Only it wasn't a cup of Gatorade or a well-timed PowerBar. It was hope from his Word found on the pages of Hebrews chapter 12.

> Since we stand surrounded by all those who have gone before, an enormous cloud of witnesses, let us drop every extra weight, every sin that clings to us and slackens our pace, and let us run with endurance the long race set before us. Now stay focused on Jesus, who designed and perfected our faith. He endured the cross and ignored the shame of that death because He focused on the joy that was set before Him; and now He is seated beside God on the throne, a place of honor (Hebrews 12:1-3 THE VOICE).

See, the Hebrew readers were weary in every way. They were losing heart fast. Some translations of this verse say they were "fainthearted," which means "cowardly, depressed, and yielding to fear."[2] Doesn't that sound like what we know about this group of readers? Does it sound a little bit like you? I guarantee you, when I read that description my heart tugged a bit. Being fainthearted is not a small thing. It can sideline the best of runners. The writer of Hebrews knew it was time to call them upward and onward. It wasn't time to quit; it was time to run. But running wasn't necessarily going to be easy or comfortable. Elisabeth Elliot agreed.

> If it's God's will that you want more than anything else in the world, it's going to mean endurance. Where did I get that idea? Isn't the Christian life supposed to be "happiness all the time, wonderful peace of mind," and feeling comfortable about things? Lots of good feelings and lots of good vibes? I heard a song about, "I love the feeling that I get when I get together with God's wonderful people." Isn't that the way it's supposed to be?
>
> Listen to what the writer to the Hebrews says: "You need endurance if you are to do God's will and attain what He has promised." You need endurance. Do you feel comfortable with that word? I don't. We like to feel comfortable about everything...How relaxed do you think Abraham felt as he toiled up that mountain with his donkey and his servant and the wood to roast his son? Relaxed? Comfortable?[3]

Enduring faith is marked by a wholehearted endeavor to run hard after Jesus. No matter what.

I think what the writer of Hebrews was saying, and what Elisabeth Elliot was getting at as well, is that if you are going to follow Jesus you need to decide ahead of time to keep going when it gets rough. Quitting is not on the table. Enduring faith is marked by a wholehearted endeavor to run hard after Jesus. No matter what.

Have you ever run hard after something? Do you know what happens when you do? Your heart is fully engaged to make sure your body has all the nutrients it needs to keep running. The harder you run, the faster your heart pumps. The same is true for us spiritually. When we set our minds to run the race of faith set before us, our hearts are fully engaged. The writer of Hebrews exhorts his readers to remember at least three things as they run hard after Jesus. This is how you grow in your endurance.

Look Back

With this historical narrative so fresh in their minds, the Hebrews really don't need a huge rehashing of what this writer just said. But the truth remains, often when we are struggling to put one foot in front of the other in our faith race, we feel alone. We think we are the only ones out on the course struggling or who have ever struggled. That simply is not the case. You and I are surrounded by a company of others who have gone before us. These "witnesses," the word *martys* in Greek, have gone before us and left a legacy for us to follow. They are not watching us—they were watching Jesus. Their lives testify to us that even in the most extreme set of circumstances you can keep running. They did, and you can too. Remember as you look back that suffering produces endurance. We can "shout our praise even when we're hemmed in with troubles, because we know how troubles can develop passionate patience in us" (Romans 5:3 MSG) just as they did for those witnesses we stand with in good company.

Lay Aside

Maybe you have made some sort of peace with the idea that to run with endurance you are going to go through a fair amount of suffering. That seems like enough of a tutor for our hearts, right? Oh, friend, if only. Next, the writer of Hebrews lets us in on another element of our training for this marathon of faith. If we are going to keep in step with Jesus, we have got to get rid of a few things. If we don't, they'll slacken our pace. I don't think we have to run in record time, but we do need to run. He said, "Let us also lay aside every weight, and sin which clings so closely, and let us run with endurance the race that is set before us"

(Hebrews 12:1). Do you want to run with endurance? We need to deal with the "weights" and the "sins" that do nothing but trip us up.

I'm going to work backward, because I feel as though we should start with the more obvious of the two: sins. It makes perfect sense to me that to be faithful, sin can't be messing up my stride. I need to cast it aside. Sin works in great effort against our endurance, and we need to get rid of it. This reminds me of when I was in high school many, many years ago. I was on summer break and a few of my friends and I were spending a leisurely day at the city swimming pool. It was perfect until I discovered an insect of epic proportion had landed on my swimsuit. This was no small critter. It was one of the evil creatures God talked about in the Bible and sent as a plague on the king of Egypt. We called them the seven-year locust. These gigantic bugs were everywhere that summer, making every kind of racket and causing small children to run inside instead of riding down the streets on their Big Wheels. I loathed them. Anyway, I did manage to make it to the pool that day and one of those nasty bugs landed on me.

As I jumped up to get into the pool, I noticed it. I may have let out a scream of death, and I cast that thing aside in a swift motion that also, much to my horror, cast aside part of my swimsuit. Quick thinking by my friends kept my modesty mostly in check, but that's a day forever engrained in my memory.

When you think of casting aside your sin, I want you to know you can't do it quick enough. It may cost you something in the process, like your pride, but it's worth it. Get rid of it, girl. And think of me with a smile when you do.

May I give you a little word of warning here as well? I know we've already discussed the whole idol thing, and you might not be in the mood for another warning quite yet, but let me just graze this one with an encouragement for you to look a little further down the passage when you get a chance. Our sin—that clings so easily to us, including the sins super hard to cast aside—draws both love and correction from our Father. This discipline is not fun and can at times be rather unpleasant. But I promise you, it comes from his loving heart and you can be sure it is for our good. He desires us to share in his holiness. Keep in mind that as you let him do that holy work of becoming like him in your heart, it will produce in you not only endurance but the peaceful fruit of righteousness (Hebrews 12:11). This is a beautiful gift, but it doesn't come easy. I love this encouragement from a commentary I read:

> The Bible is a brutally honest book. It contains stories of liars, murderers, and adulterers; and these are the good guys. If we read the Bible looking only for positive role models, we'll be quickly disappointed. But if we are honest with ourselves and confess our own faults we will find in Scripture, particularly in the First Testament, that we have much in common with many broken saints of the past. But we must not stay broken. We must follow their repentance and faith. Repentance means a change of heart, a change of mind, and ultimately a change of how we live. God's grace comes to us and enables us to turn away from sin and turn back to Him.[4]

We can't run if we are broken. Let his grace change the way you live and let it give you the strength to run.

Oh, girls, we can't run if we are broken. Let his grace change the way you live and let it give you the strength to run.

While I'm sure you're still smiling about my unfortunate swimsuit incident in the summer of 1988, let me add a bit of trivia to the mix. Did you know runners around the year this letter was written (just before AD 70) ran sans clothing? Yes. They didn't want to be bothered or weighted down with the fashionable tunics of the day. They laid aside important things like clothing to run faster. Of course, if I were a runner in that day, running naked would definitely keep my pace brisk for obvious reasons. But remember what the writer of Hebrews said: "Let us also lay aside every weight and sin."

We need to consider this for a moment or two as well. The "weights" he is implying we need to lay aside aren't necessarily sin. They may be good things (like clothing—okay, that doesn't apply today). My friend Katie says, "The seemingly harmless, even good, everyday gifts and responsibilities can rob energy from our journey toward intimacy with God."[5] You mean good things can rob me of my endurance and intimacy with God? The truth is good things can keep us from running the race God has set before us too. Sometimes deciding to lay aside good things for God's best can be even more painful than casting off the sins that easily cling to us.

My daughter Abby is a brilliant artist. I have no idea how she sketches and creates such beautiful masterpieces. My artistic talent begins and ends with staying in the lines of my adult coloring book. Clearly, she doesn't get her gift from me. Recently I came across a story about an unbelievable artist named Lilias Trotter. I thought maybe Abby might enjoy it too. Plus, Lilias was a writer as well, so both of us would be inspired. As it turned out, this story is a beautiful illustration of laying aside good things to run hard after Jesus. The documentary[6] is titled *Many Beautiful Things* and details her life as both an artist and missionary to Northern Africa.[7]

Lilias was born July 14, 1853, to a well-to-do family living in London's West End. She enjoyed the privileges this life brought her, including a private education and extensive travel. At a young age she showed an interest in spiritual things, and her understanding of God was greatly influenced by "the deeper-life conferences held at Broadlands, Oxford and Brighton, which developed into the permanent Keswick Conferences...Hungry for nourishment that would draw Lilias closer to her heavenly Father, she found her understanding of Christian faith and practice clarified and solidified, and 'the rudder of her will was set' toward God's purposes."[8] She passionately pursued a life of service with a keen heart to help the poor, especially women who worked as prostitutes, helping them secure honest employment.

A self-taught artist, she also had an eye for the beauty all around her. During a trip to Venice with her mother, she had a chance meeting with famous artist John Ruskin. After seeing her talent and precise watercolor work, he agreed to serve as her mentor. "Ruskin guided her on sketching expeditions, inviting her to study with him when they returned to England. Quickly he became convinced she possessed a rare artistic talent, which, if cultivated, would make her one of England's 'greatest living artists.'"⁹

While she accepted his invitation, and became a model student to his artistic expertise, her spiritual life also grew. Ruskin became frustrated that her ministry was taking her away from her art. He issued her an ultimatum. "He would assist her career to the highest level—but she must wholly dedicate herself to art."¹⁰ She was torn between her love for the Lord, his calling on her life, and her obvious God-given gift of artistic expression. Would she serve God best through her paintbrush? Or should she instead pour her passionate pursuit into serving others?

She prayed and wrestled deeply with her decision. Ruskin, for his part, continued to pressure her toward what he believed to be a life of a master artist. I found it interesting that during this time of struggle, Ruskin noted in one of his letters to her that her art was filled with grays and blacks and had no life in them. He felt that if she left ministry, the light would come back in her life. She knew the answer to be quite the opposite.

In the end, Lilias believed if she was going to seek the kingdom of God wholeheartedly, then she could not pursue becoming one of England's "greatest living artists." She wrote,

> Never has it been so easy to live in half a dozen harmless worlds at once—art, music, social science, games, motoring, the following of some profession, and so on. And between them we run the risk of drifting about, the good hiding the best. It is easy to find out whether our lives are focused, and if so, where the focus lies. Where do our thoughts settle when consciousness comes back in the morning? Where do they swing back when the pressure is off during the day? Dare to have it out with God, and ask Him to show you whether or not all is focused on Christ and His Glory. Turn your soul's vision to Jesus, and look

and look at Him, and a strange dimness will come over all
that is apart from Him.[11]

> She saw the good hiding the best, and by faith
> dared to fix her eyes on the one thing that
> truly mattered—Jesus and his glory.

She saw the good hiding the best, and by faith dared to fix her eyes
on the one thing that truly mattered—Jesus and his glory. Lilias left
England in 1888 and traveled with two other women to Africa to live in
Algiers and work alongside the North African Mission (although not in
an official capacity; she was rejected because of her health). "She eventually settled in the Arab section of Casbah. For the next forty years
Lilias established stations along the coast of North Africa and deeper
south in the Sahara Desert. At her death in 1928, she had established
thirteen missions and oversaw the Algiers Mission Band. During her
career she pioneered means, methods, and materials to reach the Arab
people."[12]

Although she left Ruskin and his challenge behind, she stayed in
contact with him for years through letters. And her art continued to
emerge in the diaries she kept while serving in Algeria. On nearly every
page she sketched and painted the beauty of the desert and its people.
The color missing during her decision-making season returned on the
other side of her obedience in vibrant golden sunsets and blue skies.
Lilias was living proof of how, "when our characters are refined, we
learn what it means to hope and anticipate God's goodness" (Romans
5:4 THE VOICE). She had laid aside the weight of something good, and
found the best in running with endurance a life made glorious only in
Christ and his calling.

Look to Jesus

It wouldn't surprise me at all if the writer of Hebrews was himself a runner. He must have already known something by experience I

discovered only a couple of years ago, thanks to my friend Krystal and the internet: The most important thing in a long run is the pace you keep. If you run too fast, you'll burn out quickly. If you run too slowly, you won't have the energy to keep going. Do you know what helps set the pace for runners? The answer is found in where they fix their eyes. I detailed this fascinating idea in my book *Hope for the Weary Mom*. Since it applies here, I wanted to share it with you as well. Plus, this idea is so good, it's worth sharing twice anyway.

> Focusing your gaze on points that are in close proximity to your current position will result in greater stress and mental fatigue...When focusing or "fixating" on a point much further away, you will find that you will run more easily and freely, and feel as though you are being pulled toward that point.[13]

A long-distance runner has one purpose—to finish the race. If she wants to finish she learns to fix her eyes straight ahead on the horizon where the finish line will come into view in due time. Believers, like runners, have something to fix their eyes on as well. It isn't a focal point on the horizon; it's a person who has run the race of faith perfectly already. Hebrews 12:2-3 says we should run our race "looking to Jesus, the founder and perfecter of our faith, who for the joy that was set before him endured the cross, despising the shame, and is seated at the right hand of the throne of God. Consider him who endured from sinners such hostility against himself, so that you may not grow weary or fainthearted."

I love this explanation of what "looking" means:

> The Greek word aphorontes, (looking) is derived from app, a prefix denoting "separation" and "horas," "to see." It carries the meaning of turning one's sight away from what originally held the attention for something else. The appeal is for the concentrated attention that is such more than a mere gaze. It describes an intense looking with the focus squarely on the object at hand (v. 2). The writer identified

the object on which we should focus our attention. Jesus is the ultimate example of one who ran with endurance, displaying a life of complete faithfulness to God.[14]

Are you struggling to keep pace in this faith race? When was the last time you gave Jesus more than a mere look? Have you turned your eyes from the world and looked at him intensely? Is he where you focus your attention? Here are few things to consider as you set your gaze upon him:

- He is the founder and perfecter of our faith. It begins and ends with him (12:2).
- He thoroughly dealt with our sin on the cross (12:2).
- He endured (for us) (12:2).
- He ignored the shame (for us) (12:2).
- He looked forward to the joy set before him (12:2).
- He endured personal attacks by sinners (for us) (12:3).
- He resisted to the point of death (he did not yield to sin—not once) (12:4).
- He mediated a better covenant. His blood spoke a better word (12:24).
- He made us part of an unshakable kingdom (12:28).

Does that make you want to keep running hard after Jesus as it does me? This group of verses was exactly what I needed this past spring when I felt like lying by the side of the road and quitting altogether. It was too much. Life was too hard. I really didn't think I had anything left to give. But then God's Word revived my heart once again. Do you know why? That is exactly what it is supposed to do. "Whatever was written in the former days was written for our instruction, that through endurance and through the encouragement of the Scriptures we might have hope" (Romans 15:4).

I think God knew we'd need to see it in black and white. I think he gave us Scripture like Hebrews 12:1-3 to remind us we have hope and that hope isn't wishful thinking. Hope is a person and he has run the race perfectly. We need only to look and fix our eyes on him, and we can run the race too.

There Is No "Easy" Button

Here we are with the cold hard truth. It is what Elisabeth Elliot told all those college students back in 1983. It is what I've learned in earnest over the past year as I received my word for the year reluctantly and then found myself embracing its thorny parts wholeheartedly. There is no "easy" button for faith. I wish I could tell you otherwise. But the longer I run this race, I don't need endurance less; I need it more.

> Girlfriend, I don't want you to feel better. I
> want you to run like the wind.

I feel since you have come this far into the book, and you haven't unfollowed me on social media yet, we can probably have a true heart-to-heart. When the hard days come, I want you to know Jesus is worth it. Yes, especially on those days. Girlfriend, I don't want you to feel better. I want you to run like the wind.

Recently I came across a blog post by Beth Moore. Her passion for Scripture inspires me. (I also love when she talks about her poufy hair. I mean, she is the ultimate girlfriend, right?) I read her words with tears in my eyes. I know she wrote them for me. I think maybe she wrote them for you too.

> You didn't know it was going to be like this. You had no idea what you'd stepped into.
>
> You think you must have done something wrong to make it this hard. When you started out, it wasn't like this. You haven't really told anyone. Or not very many. Mainly because you're too embarrassed.

You have no idea that every other person worth his/her salt in the kingdom of the living Christ is either going to go through their own version of the same thing or they are enduring it that very minute.

And it is hellacious...

You have come of age.

What you're going through is how it goes. I don't know why on earth we older ones are not telling you more often and with more volume. Maybe it's because we don't want to discourage you but it's so ridiculous because you're already discouraged. Or maybe it's that you won't listen to us anyway.

But this is my shot at it today. You have come of age. You have come of notice to the devil. At the same time, your very faithful God who loves you has made a covenant through the cross of Christ not only to save you but to conform you to the image of His Son. His obligation out of His wonderful grace is to grow you up. *And there is suffering in growing up.*[15]

Oh, friend, you are growing up. God loves you so much he is making you just like his Son. He is doing this absolutely with every bit of grace he can pour out over your heart. Are you discouraged today? This race is (to put it in Beth's words) "hellacious" at times. Endurance is not for the faint of heart. I don't know your story. I don't know what your endurance looks like today. But if it is anything like mine, I know you need one final bit of encouragement. You are not alone.

Keep your eyes on Jesus, who both began and finished this race we're in. Study how he did it. Because he never lost sight of where he was headed—that exhilarating finish in and with God—he could put up with anything along the way: Cross, shame, whatever. And now he's there, in the place of honor, right alongside God. When you find yourselves flagging in your faith, go over that story again, item by item, that long litany of hostility he plowed through. That will shoot adrenaline into your souls! (Hebrews 12:1-3 MSG).

This is our story. This is our anthem for the days we really want to quit. We need to burn it into our hearts line by line because this is what is going to make the difference on the hard days. You are going to need to remember to look back, lay aside whatever is holding you back (good or bad), and keep looking to Jesus every minute. He has not left us in the dust. He has paved the way. He has crossed the finish line first and is seated at the right hand of God.

And our God is a consuming fire.

Looking Forward

Hebrews 13; Hebrews 10:22-25; Revelation 19:6-7

If you were here with me now, possibly enjoying a piece of my favorite cheesecake and a truly stellar cup of coffee, I would want to see how you are really doing and if anything you've come across in this conversation about Hebrews has landed in your heart. One of my greatest joys is to listen to what women say about what they are learning and reading. In this place God usually taps me on the shoulder and says, "See that? That is the heart of a girl I love. Get to know her." I love it when he does that.

At some point you would need to eat your cheesecake, too, and since I have already polished off my piece I want to tell you something that's on my heart. I want to look you in the eyes and say, "We can't quit now. We have to finish this." I wouldn't be talking about the cheesecake or the conversation. The finish line is so close. Can't you see it? Runners usually get a second wind when they see the balloons at the end of a race. Just consider this pep talk for the last few meters of the race your balloons. A race that today includes cheesecake, which is my kind of race.

This reminds me of a story from the 2016 Summer Olympics in Rio. And if we were together I would ask you if you heard about runners Abbey D'Agostino and Nikki Hamblin. Abbey and Nikki were running a qualifying race for the 5,000 meters when they collided with about 2,000 meters to go. This kind of thing is common during races. But what happened next became the real story.

> New Zealand runner Nikki Hamblin was lying on the track, dazed after a heavy fall and with her hopes of an Olympic medal seemingly over. Suddenly, there was a hand on her shoulder and a voice in her ear: "Get up. We have to finish this."
>
> It was American Abbey D'Agostino, offering to help.
>
> "I was like, 'Yup, yup, you're right. This is the Olympic Games. We have to finish this,' Hamblin said."[1]

Nikki went down hard and Abbey wasn't about to let her just lie there. She could have run off without her, but instead she bent down, touched Nikki, and offered to help her get up, telling her to keep running. They had never met before this moment.

Nikki got up and together the two took off running. But soon it became apparent that Abbey D'Agostino was hurt worse than Nikki Hamblin. Her ankle had been injured in the fall. Did she give up at this point? I mean, surely you can't run on a bad ankle? Nope, not this girl: "Grimacing, she refused to give up, though, running nearly half the race with the injury. Hamblin did what she could, hanging back with D'Agostino for a little while to return the favor and offer encouragement."[2]

Hamblin tried to help, but eventually she had to run ahead, figuring D'Agostino would have to quit. But when Nikki reached the finish line she turned around and saw Abbey was still running—or trying to. She waited for her to cross the finish line and hugged her. Cue the tears of millions of Olympic viewers and the topic of conversation around breakfast tables around the world the next day.

Although both runners finished beyond the necessary qualifying times to reach the finals, Olympic officials gave them each a spot in the race, which would be run on Friday of that week. Unfortunately, Abbey D'Agostino was too injured to run. But because of their stunning display of sportsmanship, they were both awarded the International Fair Play Committee Award by the International Olympic Committee, an honor handed out only 17 other times in the history of the games. Later during an interview with the pair, Nikki was quoted:

> "I'm never going to forget that moment," Hamblin said. "When someone asks me what happened in Rio in 20 years' time, that's my story...That girl shaking my shoulder, [saying] 'come on, get up.'"[3]

This, my sweet sister in Christ...this is what I want you to know. I am not giving up on this race of faith. I'm going to run even if I'm bruised because I know without a shadow of doubt that Jesus is worth it. And if I happen to run by and see you have fallen to the ground, I will be the one who shakes you by the shoulders and says, "Come on, get up...we have to finish this." And then we will look forward to the finish line, together.

Four Ways to Look Forward

Part of what motivated Abbey and Nikki to keep going was the finish line. They knew it was there just ahead of them and it held a powerful pull in their runners' hearts. That same picture of the finish line gripped my heart when I first sat down to study Hebrews. You may recall that I was in a pit of despair at the time. I would certainly say I felt as though I had fallen flat to the ground right before the study started. My friend Lisa was the one saying to my heart, "Stacey, get up." I'm forever grateful she didn't just jog by. After being in the class for a few weeks, I wrote a note to my leader, Melinda, and thanked her for teaching us. I signed the letter, "Looking Forward," but at the time didn't think much of it.

The next week in class Melinda made mention of the note to the women in my study group. She said, "Girls, this is what Hebrews is saying. 'Look forward' to the finish line no matter what." From that day on, I have signed most every note or email I write with the words *looking forward* to remind myself where we are running and who is waiting for us. As I look back at our time together in this book, we have four things we can remember to do just that. I love that the writer of Hebrews made it easy for us and put them all together in a group of verses from chapter 10.

> Let us draw near with true hearts full of faith, with hearts rinsed clean of any evil conscience, and with bodies cleansed with pure water. Let us hold strong to the confession of our hope, never wavering, since the One who promised it to us is faithful. Let us consider how to inspire each other to greater love and to righteous deeds, not forgetting to gather as a community, as some have forgotten, but encouraging each other, especially as the day of His return approaches (Hebrews 10:22-25 THE VOICE).

Remember to Draw Near

If we are going to keep looking forward, we have to develop the habit of drawing near. What does it mean to draw near? It means to simply approach God and commit to know him better each day. This theme is so important that it's repeated over and over in the letter to the Hebrews. Remember, we already talked about some of these. The writer says,

- *Draw near* without fear (4:16).
- Jesus is able to save those who *draw near* (7:25).
- The law doesn't save those who *draw near* (10:1).
- *Drawing near* demonstrates our faith (11:6).

If you want to look forward every day with courage, draw near.

The Hebrews no longer had a barrier to draw near to God because Jesus, their Great High Priest, had made a way for them by his blood. "Jesus by His blood gives us courage to enter the most holy place" (10:19

THE VOICE). They didn't have to cower in the outer courts anymore. "Come," he said. They had courage given to them by Christ. And so do we. Drawing near is the application of all we have learned in this study. Don't miss this. If you want to look forward every day with courage, draw near.

Do you remember the woman made well in chapter 1? Do you know what she had the courage to do in her defining moment? She drew near and she was healed. Like her, we have the fullest confidence to draw near because we know what Christ alone has done for us. He has purified us and cleansed us. He has already made us well. Whole. Oh, girls, don't miss this for a minute. You have been given an "audience and acceptance" in Christ.[4] Make it your daily habit to come to the throne of grace and receive the grace and mercy he has to offer you (4:16). He is pouring it out abundantly and we have no excuse not to come. This is our invitation and it is glorious. Can you think of one good reason not to draw near?

Remember to Hold Fast

The writer exhorts us to hold fast or "strong" to the confession of our hope once we draw near and our hearts are reminded of every treasure we have in Jesus. I love the J. B. Phillips translation of this verse (10:23): "In this confidence let us hold on to the hope that we profess without the slightest hesitation—for he is utterly dependable." We should not have the slightest bit of hesitation because Jesus is faithful and that faithfulness should fuel ours.

> God has made great and precious promises to believers, and he is a faithful God, true to his word; there is no falseness with him, and there should be none with us. His faithfulness should excite and encourage us to be faithful, and we must depend more upon his promises to us than our promises to him, and we must plead with him the promise of grace sufficient.[5]

Now that you know, do not let go of the hope you have in Christ. Even on the days you think about losing your grip, he will not for one minute let go of you. This reminds me of when my older girls were little and I walked with them at the mall. I asked them to hold on to my shirt because I was usually pushing their little sisters in a stroller. They would hold on for the most part, but inevitably some sparkly thing would catch their eyes and they would start to drift. I would stop, get down to their eye level, and remind them they were to hold on to me no matter what. But let's face it, they needed more than a fair bit of reminding. Now, when the mall was exceptionally busy, for instance during the holidays, I wouldn't chance letting them hold on to my shirt. I would grab their little hands, put them on the stroller, and cover them with my own. I would hold on to them, because I wasn't going to lose them.

> Jesus stays. He holds. You can too.

Think for a minute of all Jesus has done to relentlessly rescue and redeem you. Hebrews 13:8 assures us "Jesus Christ is the same yesterday and today and forever." The hope you have was bought with a great price and his constancy is our confidence. Many times other "sparkly" things will try to woo you away from him. The enemy of your souls will come against you and try to convince you to let go.

Don't for one minute loosen your grip. But if, like my girls' hands did, your hand tries to wriggle free, be sure of this one thing: He will never leave you or forsake you (13:5). This happens to be one of my favorite promises in Scripture. The original language uses three negatives and says it like this: "Never will I leave you, never, never will I forsake you." Under what circumstance will Jesus leave you? Never. Jesus is the ultimate in staying. He has community with you and you have community with him. He is never leaving you. Hold fast, girlfriend, to this truth. Let it be what brings life to your soul as you walk by faith. Jesus stays. He holds. You can too.

Remember to Love One Another

One of my greatest passions is to encourage others. I guess you might say my years as a cheerleader stuck with me. I'm not talking about popularity contests or short skirts. What has stuck with me is a desire to be in your corner. I want to pull out my megaphone and yell for you to keep going. But when I'm in the midst of a trial, it's easier to pull inward and nurse my own wounded soul. My stress behavior, if you care to know, is to act fine and simultaneously cave far inside my own heart.

During these times, it's hard for me to want people around me, let alone be overjoyed to crawl outside myself and encourage them. I might even whine a little bit for others to come and cheer me up. On those days, I forget I'm surrounded by people who might be hurting too. I think we all do this, don't we? The writer of Hebrews knew it too. He spent the first 12 chapters speaking for the most part to the individual believers, but in the last chapter of Hebrews, in his final few sentences, he makes a point to remind them not to neglect one another and the body of believers around them. He exhorts them to make marriage a priority (because it should be tops), respect their leaders who pour out the Word of God, care for those in prison (as if you are their cellmate) and "never let [their] brotherly love fail" (13:1 PHILLIPS).

Why? Because trials will come. We have this as a guarantee. The world will not come running to our rescue. If you recall, they killed our liberator (Hebrews 13:12-13). We are going to need one another more than we know. Therefore, he reminds the Hebrews to "consider how to inspire each other to greater love and to righteous deeds, not forgetting to gather as a community, as some have forgotten, but encouraging each other" (Hebrews 10:24-25 THE VOICE). Do it like it is your job, because it is. I love this quote by my friends at She Reads Truth:

> We are all bridesmaids for each other. The women in your life are the bride of Christ. And we are headed to the marriage supper of the Lamb (Rev 19:6-9). Therefore, we are called to help the bride get ready for the wedding.[6]

What a beautiful description of how we are to inspire and encourage one another. It made me think about my five beautiful bridesmaids who stood with me on April 23, 1994. According to my daughter,

Emma, they must have been true friends, because I made them wear the ugliest dresses ever created. I tried to tell her it was the nineties and she really had no clue what was "in." She rolled her eyes as all teenagers do at one point or another. I have to admit she was right about one thing: These women were the ones I wanted to encourage me on Mike's and my special day.

For starters, they said yes to those "ugly" green floral print dresses. They cleared their schedules and they came. They showed up. They prayed for me, they brought me real Coca-Cola, and they fed me health food like Twizzlers. They laughed with me when I was nervous. And they helped avert my big crisis of the day. You know there is always at least one crisis on your wedding day, right? Mine was the bridesmaids' bouquets. I had a vision and I thought my florist was on board. I wanted a sweet bundle of wildflowers with three large Gerber daisies in the faintest color of blush in the center.

The flowers arrived at the church the morning of the wedding and I found myself next to tears. The Gerber daises were there all right, but they were sprayed florescent pink. They had to have been individually colored with painstaking care; flowers of this color do not occur in nature. I mean, why would God choose that color for his beautiful display of glory? No, he did not. But for some reason, my florist thought they would match my other splashes of blush perfectly. Instead, when my girls grabbed their flowers with wary eyes, all I could see was "1980s Hot Pink Flowers" getting all the attention. The problem was, they were the main part of the bouquet. At this point I could not make another rational decision, except to say "I do" in about an hour's time. My bridesmaids gathered in a circle and worked their magic. They yanked those daisies out so fast you couldn't tell they were ever part of their bouquets. And when they turned around to show me what they had re-created, they each had stuck their florescent pink daisies down the center of their "ugly" dresses, as if to say, "Stacey, this is what matters. Forget the flowers. We are here for you."

I doubled over laughing and the daisies went into the trash. No one who came to the wedding feast of Kentucky Fried Chicken that day (so not kidding about this) was ever suspicious my flowers had been an issue at all.

> Is the bride thinking about quitting or running the other way? Encourage her and remind her she is beautiful because of Christ.

This is what we need to be doing for one another. Is the bride thinking about quitting or running the other way? Inspire her to keep going. Is she weeping in the corner messing her makeup and soiling her pretty dress? Encourage her and remind her she is beautiful because of Christ. Does she feel alone? Gather, girls. Gather around tables filled with yummy treats and open the Word of God between you. Pour out the true encouragement written especially for her heart by the One who loves her more than she will ever be able to comprehend—her groom. He is her beloved and she is his. Oh, friend, serve and love his bride.

Remember Your Reward Is Coming

The reason we need to keep looking forward is that our reward is coming. The finish line is not so very far away. I promise it is just around the corner, and even if you can't see it quite yet, we have the full assurance that it is real and we know who is waiting for us. Let's return to the wedding-day theme and what every bride is looking forward to. She is looking for her groom.

Unfortunately, the church I got married in did not have a center aisle. I was so deeply distraught by this as a girl growing up. But you know what? On the day of my wedding, even though I couldn't see Mike, I knew he was there. He promised me he would be. My bridesmaids all made it down the aisle with their simplified bouquets and none of them came running back to tell me anything different. I grabbed my daddy's arm, he smiled, and we walked down the aisle with confidence, knowing my groom was ready. He was waiting for me and had eyes only for me. Remember the verse from the quote above?

Praise the Lord!
For the Lord our God,
   the All Powerful, reigns supreme.
Now is the time for joy and happiness.
   He deserves all the glory we can give Him.
For the wedding feast has begun; the marriage of the Lamb to
His bride has commenced,
   and His bride has prepared herself for this glorious day."
   (Revelation 19:6-7 the voice).

Someday we will all be together around the throne, laughing and singing and enjoying forever. The sound will be glorious. In the meantime, do not abandon your hope. Do not forget to remind your fellow bridesmaids either. Tell them, "Don't throw away your trust now—it carries a rich reward in the world to come" (Hebrews 10:35 phillips). Jesus is there and he has eyes for only his bride. What a day of rejoicing that will be.

Pray for Me; I'll Pray for You

I have heard it said, "Nothing makes you love a person more than praying for them." I think that is absolutely true. I dearly love those I pray for. But I also happen to think the reverse is true: "Nothing makes you pray for a person more than loving them." We pray like crazy for those we love best. They are the list. I know we pray for others who cross our paths randomly, and we should. But we go to the floor and kneel for those we love passionately, and we love passionately those who are willing to kneel on our behalf. I think the writer to the Hebrews loved them like this. And he wasn't afraid to ask them to pray for him too. He said, "Pray for us, for we are sure that we have a clear conscience, desiring to act honorably in all things. I urge you the more earnestly to do this in order that I may be restored to you the sooner" (13:18-21). I think he knew this to be true:

If we are honest, we have to admit that coming to Jesus and entering His church ruins us—at least as far as this world is concerned. If we identify with Him in His suffering and rejection, we become a reproachful irritation to the powers that rule this culture. If we ever felt at home in this world—if we ever sensed we belonged—then we would wake up one day to discover that we will never be at home again until we enter the city of God. By entering through Jesus, we become citizens of another city, subjects of another king. As long as we are here, we should live as resident aliens longing to go home.[7]

> We need to pray for one another. It is one of the ways we love each other well. Love well and pray often.

We are ruined for this world with a deep longing to go home. We need to pray for one another. It is one of the ways we love each other well. Love well and pray often. I was part of a gathering of women not too long ago that started out as encouragement for weary moms. My friend and coauthor of *Hope for the Weary Mom*, Brooke McGloth-lin, was in town, and some of my local friends were excited to meet her for the first time. We sent out invitations and spent a couple of hours together. It was a sweet evening to be sure. First, I don't get to see Brooke very often. Second, we drank my favorite coffee. But most of all we shared hope, which as you know I love to talk about.

Toward the end of the evening one of the women had a prayer need. This precious single mom of four was having surgery in the morning and facing a difficult journey in the days ahead. We asked her to come forward and began to pray over her. The day before I had been reminded that God is good and we need to trust him to be good to us. A friend had sent me the words to a song by Chris Tomlin titled "Good Good Father" when I needed it most. When it was my turn to pray, I borrowed some of the language of that song and prayed.

I cried. This mom cried. As did every other woman in the room. We ugly cried and cried out to Jesus to heal our friend. But then it happened before we knew it. My friend Angie felt a nudge by the Lord, and she started singing that song. Her stunning alto voice sang the first line and then she asked us to join her. Every tear-filled woman did just that. Right there in my friend Erin's family room we prayed, we loved, and we worshiped our good, good Father. The next day I received a message from that sweet mom. The praise in her heart as she was going into surgery was that God was good. She was trusting him to be good to her. And he was.

In the middle of asking his friends to pray for him, the writer of Hebrews breaks out into a prayer of his own for them. A heart for prayer can't help but pray. I think it is one of the most beautiful benedictions in the New Testament.

> May the God of peace, who brought the great Shepherd of the sheep, our Lord Jesus, back from the dead through the blood of the new everlasting covenant, perfect you in every good work as you work God's will. May God do in you only those things that are pleasing in His sight through Jesus the Anointed, our Liberating King, to whom we give glory always and forever. Amen" (Hebrews 13:20-21 THE VOICE).

> Maturity does not come through our own striving. It comes as we allow Christ to work in us through the power of his Word.

How are we going to make it in this world we don't belong in? We are going to trust the God of peace to do those things in us that are pleasing in his sight—*through Jesus*. Maturity does not come through our own striving. It comes as we allow Christ to work in us through the power of his Word. And we know he is able to do far more than we ask or imagine because he brought our great Shepherd, our liberating King, back from the dead (Ephesians 3:20). God is the one who works in you, and he gets all the glory.

I want you to know this is my greatest prayer for you, my sweet friend. I promise you are on my list. I see you at church, cruising on

Facebook, and smiling back at me on Instagram with your giant cups of coffee. I bump into you at conferences and on occasion at the grocery store. I pray for you; I truly do. Most days I do so with tears streaming down my face because I love you like crazy.

As we close the pages of this book, this is what is on my heart: I know sometimes it seems all the world is doing its level best to derail you. Well-meaning people may convince you to stop running. Oh, sweet friend, get up! *You don't want to miss this!* And if by chance you are contemplating throwing in the towel altogether, don't do it. Instead, draw near. Hold fast. Love one another. Look forward.

And from start to finish, worship with your whole heart.

> Through Jesus, then, let us keep offering to God our own sacrifice, the praise of lips that confess His name without ceasing...Jesus the Anointed, our Liberating King, to whom we give glory always and forever. Amen...May grace always be with you" (Hebrews 13:15,21,25 THE VOICE).

A Small Guide for Small Groups

One of my favorite things in life is gathering a small group of women to dive deep into heart-to-heart conversations. Years ago I took part in such a group. We focused on God's Word but also read books that went along with what we were studying in Scripture. Our meetings proved to be some of the sweetest times I have spent around a table as we shared honestly about life, grew in our faith, and prayed for one another.

I would be crazy honored if you chose to do something similar with *Is Jesus Worth It?* I think it has the potential to connect the hearts of women in an authentic way. As you read this book together, you will also be going through the book of Hebrews. I think that makes a perfect combination. Might I make a couple of gentle suggestions to leaders if you are planning to embark on a small-group study?

1. **Ground the study in God's Word.** Each chapter has verses and stories participants can find in their Bibles. Ask them to bring their Bibles with them each week. Choose a section of Scripture to read aloud with your group. Then let God's living and active Word do its work in yielded hearts and open minds.

2. **Bathe your group in prayer.** Start now. Ask God to lead you to the women he wants you to invite. Pray as you read

through this book and highlight discussion points. Pray
when you gather. Be committed to praying for one another
between meetings. Begin and end your time with prayer.

3. **Find a co-leader (and perhaps a hostess).** Don't attempt
to lead a group of women alone. God made us to need one
another in the most beautiful way. I find if you lead one
week and your partner leads the next week, you will have a
chance to sit back and minister in an entirely different way.
Also, you might invite a third person to be hostess. Find
someone who has the gift of hospitality, and her gifts will
shine as women are offered beverages and treats during
your time together. Having a separate hostess will bless the
women who attend and bless you.

4. **Plan to meet for no more than six or seven weeks.** (Let
women know upfront how many weeks are involved
so they can arrange their schedules to be present. Most
women could join you for six nights of discussion.) This
book has ten chapters. You can easily meet one time to get
to know one another, and then cover about two chapters
each week for five or six weeks. When you are finished,
you might decide to take a break or pick another book.

5. Each chapter in the small-group study guide follows the
same format:

- *Encouragement* from God's Word. Sometimes I'll
ask you to read the entire chapter from the book of
Hebrews that week's discussion is based on, but at least
specific verses you'll focus on during group time.

- *Connection* through discussion. The women should
also be ready to recite the suggested memorized Scripture aloud during the following week's discussion. I
find that when they know they'll have to recite Scripture to the group, memorizing becomes a higher priority. Also, as you memorize together, the Scripture

becomes even more meaningful. Tell them to relax, assuring them that the others will cheer them on and even help them if they suddenly forget and are completely wordless!

- *Growth* with life application. I like to have women highlight the three or four statements in each chapter that are most significant to them. They should be prepared to share one of their favorites and why it spoke to them. This makes for a deep and meaningful discussion.

6. Do me a favor, please. Email me at stacey@staceythacker .com and let me know your group is meeting. I'd love to pray for you and answer any questions you might have.

Start with Worship

Encouragement

Read Hebrews 1 and focus on Hebrews 1:1-3.

Connection

1. What can you learn from the unnamed, faceless woman who reached out to touch Jesus's hem in Matthew 9:20-22? Do you think she thought Jesus was worth it?

2. Think about the last thing you thought you wanted. Was it a day at the spa, a new cardigan, or a date with a special someone? Did it bring you satisfaction of a lasting kind? Was that satisfaction sustainable over days and weeks? Or did it fade and you found your heart longing for something else to replace it?

3. True worship deeply humbles us, just as it did Isaiah. He saw the Lord and knew immediately he was not worthy of the calling on his life to serve God. How many times have you gone through the motions of worship but not let God humble you? Why do you think so often we merely go through the motions? Tell about a time when true worship deeply humbled your heart.

Growth

1. Do you need to sit and receive the finished work of Jesus today? Do you need to remember he holds on no matter what? Take your moment, friend. Sit and receive.

2. Memorize Hebrews 1:3 to share next week.

2

Fear(less)

Encouragement

Read Hebrews 2 and focus on Hebrews 2:1-4 and 14-18.

Connection

1. What fear has been bossing you around lately? When will that fear lose its power and slink away from you? Be bold and say to one another, "Your fear [name it] has no power in the presence of Jesus." You might say it like this: "Robin, your fear of rejection has no power in the presence of Jesus."

2. What does Hebrews 2:1-4 tells us to pay close attention to? Why is it important to being fear(less)?

3. How does the gospel change us? What is the ultimate end or goal of the gospel?

Growth

1. Read through the prayer at the end of this chapter. Write your own response or use this one as you thank God for the power of the gospel to change us and make us fear(less).

2. Memorize Hebrews 2:14-15 to share next week.

3. Make a commitment this week to pay close attention to the truths you are learning as you study God's Word. One way to remember what you're learning is to tell someone else. Think of one friend or family member who needs to be reminded about the power of the gospel and share that reminder with them.

Abraham to Anchors

Encouragement

Read Hebrews 6 and focus on Hebrews 6:19-20.

Connection

1. Why was Abraham the perfect choice to illustrate moving forward in faith for the Hebrews? What did he represent to them?

2. Abraham was not perfectly obedient. He experienced a long gap of time between the promise from God and its fulfillment in his life. What was God doing during that time? How does this encourage you?

3. What is hope and where does it lead us?

Growth

1. What backstory has God been weaving into your life? Take time this week to journal through your story and look for God working in the midst of it. How might God use your story in the life of someone else?

2. Suffering. Endurance. Character. This is God's classroom. And it produces hope. Reflect honestly on where you are today. Will you by faith move on to maturity?

3. Memorize Hebrews 6:19-20 to share next week.

The Word

Encouragement

Read Hebrews 4 and focus on Hebrews 4:12-16.

Connection

1. When was the last time you took a long drink of the living water of the Word? What part of Scripture were you reading or studying?

2. Why do you think maturity and God's Word go hand in hand?

3. Which part of the description of God's Word in Hebrews 4:12 speaks to your heart most right now? Living? Active? Sharp?

Growth

1. This week work through the LIFE study plan for Hebrews 4:14-16. Take a little time each day to Listen, Investigate, Face-to-Face, or Experience it in real life. You might try "Listen" on Monday, "Investigate" on Tuesday, and so forth. Come to group time ready to talk about how God's Word brought you LIFE this week!

2. Memorize Hebrews 4:12 to share next week.

Your Great High Priest

Encouragement

Read Hebrews 5:1-10 and Hebrews 7:1–8:5,9.

Connection

1. How do you feel about this?: "Once you know the truth, you are responsible for it." Now look at each woman at the table and tell her you are committed to helping her be responsible for the truth you are learning together. Then ask her to do the same for you. This is what girlfriends do for each other.

2. What is the purpose of the Great High Priest?

3. Why is Jesus a better high priest and the only one we need?

Growth

1. Is it hard for you to imagine that Jesus is praying for you? Why or why not?

2. John 17 reveals the heart of your rescuer, your Great High Priest. What have you learned about his heart for you?

3. Memorize Hebrews 7:25 to share.

Unshakable

Encouragement

Read Hebrews 3:1-6 and Hebrews 8:6-12.

Connection

1. What stories did your family tell around the dinner table? What stories do you tell your children or other children in your life over and over?

2. Compare Moses and Jesus. Why is Jesus worthy of more glory?

3. Did God's Beloved stay constant? Look at 2 Kings 17:40-41. How does this stir your heart?

Growth

1. What are you still holding onto that Christ's death on the cross destroyed?

2. When was the last time you quietly, patiently, and with a determined concentration tried to discover all you could possibly know about Jesus?

3. Look at the list of questions on page 107 and take a few moments to do a heart check. You might write them on a note card and tuck them into your Bible or purse to re-visit them.

4. Memorize Hebrews 3:1 to share.

The Cease to Do

Encouragement

Read Hebrews 3:7–4:11.

Connection

1. What habit did Israel continually fall into and why?

2. What is rest? How does God view rest? Why is it important that we "enter" the rest he has for us?

3. Of the three truths about rest (it is his rest, rest remains open to us, and God prepared the place of rest himself), which one speaks to your heart the most? What are you struggling with today?

Growth

1. Using Listen, Position, and Linger, spend some time considering what idols you most struggle with and why. Perhaps you aren't struggling with keeping and doing like me, but something else entirely. I hope my story will encourage you to seek the Lord and let him do the work he so desperately wants to do in your heart. Know I'm praying for you.

2. Memorize Hebrews 3:13 to share.

Faithful

Encouragement

Read Hebrews 11.

Connection

1. What is faith? What is your favorite truth about faith found in this chapter?

2. Have you had your fill of soul-empty people? (God bless Habakkuk!) What does a firm look at Jesus and his life show us about faith?

3. Why are these names included in the hall of faith? What have you learned about them that you didn't know before?

Growth

1. Look at this chapter with fresh eyes. I was fascinated by Jochebed, the mother of Moses. (I know. You didn't see that coming, did you?) Pick one name from the hall of faith and do a deeper study this week. Ask God to encourage you through his Word as you dig into the life of one called "faithful."

2. Memorize Hebrews 11:1 to share. (If you already know it, try a different translation.)

The One Thing You're Really Going to Need

Encouragement

Read Hebrews 12.

Connection

1. Do you have a word for the year? Share it with the group and tell what you have learned.

2. According to Elisabeth Elliot, if God's will is what you want more than anything else, what are you going to need?

3. How do you grow in endurance according to Hebrews 12:1-3?

Growth

1. Oh, sweet friend. I wish I could tell you there was really an "easy" button for this walk of faith. But we both know there is not. Grab your journal. It's time for you to write out exactly what is on your heart. Before we go one step more, tell Jesus. Tell him where your heart is today. Pray over those words. Weep if you need to. But know that as you grow up into him there will be hard days. But you are not alone. (If you feel comfortable doing so, share part of what you wrote with the group. No pressure, of course, but I find in these hard places hearts truly connect. Be brave. Together.)

2. Memorize Hebrews 12:1-2 to share.

Looking Forward

Encouragement

Read Hebrews 13 and Hebrews 10:22-25.

Connection

1. What part of this book study on Hebrews has really landed in your heart? What parts have worked their way past your heart and into your daily conversations with your friends and family?

2. When and why are you tempted to give up on the race of faith? What makes a difference to keep you running? Have you ever had someone say, "Come on, get up. Keep running!"?

3. How can we love each other well? Who can you be a "bridesmaid" for today?

4. Spend time praying together.

Growth

1. How will you commit from today forward to make it a habit to draw near?

2. Remember today, tomorrow, and always Jesus will hold on to you. He will never let you go. Take time to thank him for that truth and hold fast to this promise each and every day.

3. Memorize Hebrews 13:15 and share it with someone who needs to hear it.

My Prayer for You

May the God of peace, who brought the great Shepherd of the sheep, our Lord Jesus, back from the dead through the blood of the new everlasting covenant, perfect you in every good work as you work God's will. May God do in you only those things that are pleasing in His sight through Jesus the Anointed, our Liberating King, to whom we give glory always and forever. Amen (Hebrews 13:20-21 THE VOICE).

A Note from Stacey

I have a rather unusual maiden name. If you were a child of the seventies (as I was), my name didn't hint at my current career as a "Christian author" but screamed "rock star groupie" instead. Let's just say that when I put it on social media recently, my friends who didn't know me as I grew up had a good laugh.

What my new friends didn't know was my maiden name gave me certain privileges growing up. At one store in town I was more than a customer. I could walk in anytime and be guaranteed a warm welcome. The salespeople knew me and often would let me come behind the counter and "help" them. It wasn't unusual for them to take my hand and lead me over to the girls' clothing section, point out a new outfit that had just arrived, and pull down my size. They knew it by heart. With my mom's nod, the outfit would be put in a special bag just for me. The bag also happened to have my last name on it. They were personal like that.

Probably the best part of my last name was that it gave me access to the secret place in the back of the store. I could (and often did) run past the perfume counter and shoes and go straight to the desk where the boss man sat. He was always impeccably dressed in a suit and tie, busy working some deal or going over the sales for the day. But since I was a welcomed guest, he never minded my interruptions. Usually, he would ask if I had found a new outfit and whether my mom was with me. Sometimes, if he wasn't too busy, he'd walk with me through the store and point out the best of what had come that day in shipment. Years later, when I was a little older, he gave me a job and usually stuffed my purse with more items than I sold.

The reason I had special access and the invitation to be more than a customer at that store is that my name was not only on the bag, but my name was also on the store marquee. My granddad owned the store and several others across the state. I carried his name not only when I walked into the store, but everywhere I went in town. So you see, not many people laughed about it back then. Growing up a *Stoner* was kind of a big deal. I was shocked when I found out not everyone had a well-known last name like mine. It was so normal for me because I was born into it.

You have a name that is kind of a big deal too. God has revealed it to us in his Word. Long ago, before he laid the foundations of the world, he was thinking about you (and me) and how much he loved us. He decided from the beginning of time to adopt us as his daughters through his only Son, Jesus. Do you know how he felt about that? He delighted in doing so. His plan was for us to be part of his special family. Being part of his family brings with it blessings of untold worth, gifts we get to experience now and forever, and more importantly access to our heavenly Father no one can hinder.

In this book one of The Girlfriend's Guide to the Bible series, we've taken a long look at Jesus in the book of Hebrews and how doing so ignites our faith. As I've thought about where we could next dive deep into the pages of God's Word, my heart has been drawn to the question we all ask at some point in our lives: "Who am I?" Often we look to the opinion of others for the answer to that question. Maybe we read self-help books to try to answer it, or we search social media for someone we want to be like and imitate them. Too often we come away feeling as though we don't measure up—mostly because we believe the lie we have to be enough in the first place.

But what does God have to say about it? Knowing his heart for us will make a world of difference in how we view ourselves and live out our story the way he planned for us to from the beginning of time.

What does he say about us?

blessed

chosen

blameless

no longer slaves

free

Doesn't that make you want to cry a little bit? When was the last time someone on Facebook called you blessed? Has anyone reminded you today you are free? Oh, my sweet friend, you are his daughter. You carry his name. You are all these things, and more.

Book two in this series will take us to the city of Ephesus, where a preacher named Timothy is doing his level best to proclaim Jesus in a dark and desperate world. His mentor, Paul, pens a letter from his jail cell and with line after line tells Timothy and his congregation about not simply who they are, but *whose* they are. Because God's living and active Word is for us, too, we get to read it knowing it is written for us. We can lean in and consider the truth of it for our hearts. And prayerfully, when we come to the end of the powerful book of Ephesians, we will know both the answer to the question, "Who do you say I am" and the glorious gift of being his girl.

Looking forward,

Stacey

Notes

Introduction

1. Flannery O'Connor, *A Prayer Journal* (New York: Farrar, Straus and Giroux, 2013), 11.

Chapter 1: Start with Worship

1. Charles Spurgeon, Preceptaustin.org, http://www.preceptaustin.org/spurgeon_sermons_on_hebrews.htm#dah, accessed 10/27/15.
2. John Piper, http://www.soundofgrace.com/piper96/03-31-96.htm, accessed 10/31/15.
3. Ibid.
4. S.V., *Charakter*, blueletterbible.org, https://www.blueletterbible.org/lang/lexicon/lexicon.cfm?Strongs=G5481&t=KJV, accessed 02/29/16.
5. Charles Spurgeon, Preceptaustin.org, http://preceptaustin.org/hebrews_18-14.htm, accessed 11/6/15.
6. Stacey Thacker, *Fresh Out of Amazing* (Eugene, OR: Harvest House Publishers, 2016), 97.
7. A.W. Tozer, *Worship: The Missing Jewel* (Camp Hill, PA: Christian Publications, Inc., June 1996), 4-5.
8. Christy Nockels, Abundance Conference, December 5, 2015.

Chapter 2: Fear(less)

1. Hannah Hurnard, *Hinds' Feet in High Places* (Blacksburg, VA: Wilder Publications, 2010), 4.
2. Ibid.
3. Matthew Henry, *Matthew Henry Commentary on the Whole Bible (Complete)*, https://www.bible gateway.com/passage/?search=hebrews+2%3A1-4&version=ESV, accessed 11/14/15.
4. Ray Stedman, blueletterbible.org, https://www.blueletterbible.org/Comm/stedman_ray/Adv_Hbr/Adv_Hbr.cfm?a=1137012, accessed 12/21/15.
5. Crystal Stine, Incourage.me, *Fervent: Strategy 6: Your Fear*, http://www.incourage.me/2016/03/fervent-strategy-6-your-fear.html, accessed 03/22/16.
6. Matthew Henry, *Matthew Henry Commentary on the Whole Bible (Complete)*, https://www.bible gateway.com/passage/?search=Phil%204%3A8-9&version=ESV, accessed 03/18/16.
7. Milton Vincent, *A Gospel Primer for Christians: Learning to See the Glories of God's Love* (Bemid-ji, MN: Focus Publishing, 2008), 54.

Chapter 3: Abraham to Anchors

1. Chuck Swindoll, *Abraham: One Nomad's Amazing Journey of Faith* (Carol Stream, IL: Tyndale Publishers, August 1, 2014), Introduction.

2. Ibid.

3. Warren Wiersbe, *Wiersbe's Expository Outlines of the New Testament* (Colorado Springs, CO: David C Cook, 1992), 674.

4. Swindoll, *Abraham: One Nomad's Amazing Journey of Faith.*

5. Henry, *Matthew Henry Commentary on the Whole Bible (Complete).* https://www.biblegateway.com/passage/?search=Heb%206%3A13-20&version=VOICE.

6. "Happy Hour" with Jamie Ivey, Episode 85, Shelley Giglio, April 20, 2016.

Chapter 4: The Word

1. Warren Wiersbe, *Wiersbe's Expository Outlines on the New Testament* (Colorado Springs, CO: David C Cook, 1992), 690.

2. Word: Blueletterbible.org, https://www.blueletterbible.org/lang/lexicon/lexicon.cfm?Strongs=G3056&t=KJV, accessed 06/23/16.

3. Living: Blueletterbible.org, https://www.blueletterbible.org/lang/lexicon/lexicon.cfm?Strongs=G2198&t=KJV, accessed 06/23/16.

4. R.C. Sproul, *Knowing Scripture* (Downers Grove: IL: InterVarsity Press, 1977), 14–15.

5. Tomos: Blueletterbible.org, https://www.blueletterbible.org/lang/lexicon/lexicon.cfm?Strongs=G5114&t=KJVm accessed 06/24/16.

6. Koptō: blueletterbible.org, https://www.blueletterbible.org/lang/lexicon/lexicon.cfm?strongs=G2875&t=KJV, accessed 06/24/16.

7. Matthew Henry, *Matthew Henry Commentary on the Whole Bible (Complete)*, https://www.biblegateway.com/passage/?search=hebrews%204%3A12&version=ESV, accessed 06/24/16.

8. Stacey Thacker, *Fresh Out of Amazing* (Eugene, OR: Harvest House Publishers, 2016), 177–78.

9. John Piper, DesiringGod.org, http://www.desiringgod.org/articles/lenten-lights, 03/24/16.

Chapter 5: Your Great High Priest

1. Dorothy Kelley Patterson, and Rhonda Harrington Kelley, *Women's Evangelical Commentary of the New Testament* (Nashville, TN: B&H Publishing Group, 2011), 763.

2. Biblegateway.com, Note from The Voice Translation on Leviticus Chapter 4, https://www.biblegateway.com/passage/?search=Leviticus%204&version=ESV;VOICE, accessed 07/04/2016.

3. Charles Spurgeon, http://www.spurgeongems.org/vols37-39/chs2251.pdf, accessed 06/30/2016.

4. Warren Wiersbe, *Wiersbe's Expository Outlines on the New Testament* (Colorado Springs, CO: David C Cook, 1992), 695–96.

5. Matthew Henry, *Matthew Henry Commentary on the Whole Bible (Complete)*, https://www.biblegateway.com/passage/?search=hebrews%207&version=ESV, accessed 07/05/2016.

6. A. W. Tozer, *Experiencing the Presence of God: Teachings from the Book of Hebrews* (Bloomington, MN: Bethany House Publishers, 2010), 60.

7. Ibid.

8. Ibid., 70–71.

9. Krista Williams, First5.org, Seated in Heavenly Places, accessed 03/31/16.

10. Patterson & Kelley, *Women's Evangelical Commentary of the New Testament*, 243.

11. Charles Spurgeon, "Our Compassionate High Priest" No. 2251, http://www.spurgeongems.org/vols37-39/chs2251.pdf, accessed 07/09/2106.

Chapter 6: Unshakable

1. Biblegateway.com, Note from The Voice Translation on Hebrews 3:1-6, https://www.biblegateway.com/passage/?search=Hebrews%203&version=VOICE, accessed 07/15/2016.

2. Ibid.

3. Robert Boyd Munger, *My Heart—Christ's Home*, Rev. Ed. (Downers Grove, IL: InterVarsity Press, 1986), 3–4.

4. The Bible Panorama Commentary: Bible Gateway, https://www.biblegateway.com/passage/?search=Heb+8%3A6-12&version=ESV, accessed 03/08/16.

5. Matthew Henry, *Matthew Henry Commentary on the Whole Bible (Complete)*, https://www.biblegateway.com/passage/?search=Heb+8&version=ESV, accessed 03/08/2016.

6. Charles R. Swindoll, *Come Before Winter and Share My Hope* (Grand Rapids, MI: Zondervan, 1994), np.

7. Henry Blackaby and Richard Blackaby, *Being Still with God Every Day* (Nashville, TN: Thomas Nelson, 2014), np.

8. Andrew Murray, *The Holiest of All: An Exposition of the Epistle to the Hebrews*, updated ed. (New Kensington, PA: Whitaker House, 2004), 103–104.

9. Kevin DeYoung, *Taking God at His Word* (Wheaton, IL: Crossway, 2014), 22.

10. Charles Spurgeon, Studylight.org, http://www.studylight.org/commentaries/spe/view.cgi?bk=heb&ch=3, accessed 11/17/15.

Chapter 7: The Cease to Do

1. Biblegateway.com, Note from The Voice Translation on Hebrews 4:5, https://www.biblegateway.com/passage/?search=Hebrews+3%3A7-4%3A11&version=ESV;VOICE, accessed 07/30/16.

2. Chuck Swindoll, *Abraham: One Nomad's Amazing Journey of Faith* (Carol Stream, IL: Tyndale House Publishers, 2014), viii.

3. S.V. "Cried", Blueletterbible.org, https://www.blueletterbible.org/lang/lexicon/lexicon.cfm?Strongs=H6817&t=KJV, accessed 07/30/16.

4. John MacArthur, Gracetoyou.org, http://www.gty.org/resources/sermons/1609/Entering-into-Gods-Rest, accessed 12/17/15.

5. Emily P. Freeman, *Grace for the Good Girl* (Grand Rapids, MI: Revel, 2011), 12.

6. Ibid., 145.

7. Ibid., 150.

8. Watchman Nee, *Sit, Walk, Stand* (Carol Stream, IL: Tyndale House Publishers, 1977), 5.

9. Ibid., 3.

10. Ibid., 4.

11. Ibid., 6.

Chapter 8: Faithful

1. H.A. Ironside, Studylight.org, http://www.studylight.org/commentaries/isn/hebrews-11.html, accessed 08/26/2016.

2. John Piper, TheSoundofGrace.com, http://www.soundofgrace.com/piper97/6-1-97.htm, accessed 08/26/2016.

3. S.V. "Faith", Blueletterbible.org, https://www.blueletterbible.org/lang/lexicon/lexicon.cfm?Strongs=G4102&t=KJV, accessed 08/26/2016.

4. Charles Spurgeon, http://www.spurgeongems.org/vols1-3/chs107.pdf, accessed 09/02/2016.

5. Bible Gateway, https://www.biblegateway.com/resources/all-women-bible/Jochebed, accessed 09/05/16.

6. S.V. "ou", Biblehub.org, http://biblehub.com/greek/3756.htm, accessed 09/05/16.

7. Katie Orr, *Everyday Faith* (Birmingham, AL: New Hope Publications, 2016), 124.

Chapter 9: The One Thing You're Really Going to Need

1. Elisabeth Elliot, Revive Our Hearts Podcast, January 6, 2016, https://www.reviveourhearts.com/radio/revive-our-hearts/gain-what-you-cannot-lose-day-1/.

2. S.V. "fainthearted," Webster's Dictionary of 1828 Online Edition, http://webstersdictionary1828.com/Dictionary/fainthearted, accessed 09/13/2016.

3. Elliot, Revive Our Hearts Podcast, January 6, 2016.

4. Commentary note on Hebrews chapter 12 (THE VOICE), https://www.biblegateway.com/passage/?search=hebrews%2012&version=VOICE, accessed 09/13/2016.

5. Orr, *Everyday Faith*, 43.

6. In the documentary, Lilias is voiced by the stunning Michelle Dockery, whom you may remember as Mary from *Downton Abbey*. By the way, I want to go on the record that if a documentary is ever made of my life, please have Michelle narrate it for me. Her voice is perfection. I think she could read the phone book and I'd be impressed.

7. *Many Beautiful Things*, documentary, Lilias Trotter, liliastrotter.com https://ililiastrotter.wordpress.com/2016/08/17/lilias-trotter-symposium/August 17, 2016.

8. Ibid.

9. Ibid.

10. Connie Ruth Christiansen, Turn Your Eyes Upon Jesus, the Song and the Story, Share Faith.Com, http://www.sharefaith.com/guide/Christian-Music/hymns-the-songs-and-the-stories/turn-your-eyes-upon-jesus-the-song-and-the-story.html, accessed 09/13/2016.

11. Ibid.

12. Lilias Trotter, liliastrotter.com, https://ililiastrotter.wordpress.com/2016/08/17/lilias-trotter-symposium/August 17, 2016.

13. Derek M. Hansen, "Where You Look Can Affect How You Look: Running Mechanics and Gaze Control," August 4, 2009, http://www.runningmechanics.com/articles/biomechanics-and-technique/where-you-look-can-affect-how-you-look-running-mechanics-and-gaze-control/.

14. Patterson & Kelley, *Women's Evangelical Commentary of the New Testament*, 784.

15. Beth Moore, http://blog.lproof.org/2016/05/to-servants-of-jesus-in-your-30s-and-40s.html, accessed 09/18/16.

Chapter 10: Looking Forward

1. "Runners Help Each Other After Fall: 'Get Up. We Have to Finish This,'" *The New York Times,* August 16, 2016, http://www.nytimes.com/2016/08/17/sports/olympics/nikki-hamblin-abbey -dagostino-womens-5000.html?_r=0.

2. Ibid.

3. Ibid.

4. Henry, *Matthew Henry Commentary on the Whole Bible (Complete),* https://www.biblegateway .com/passage/?search=Hebrews%2010%3A19-26&version=ESV, accessed 09/27/2016.

5. Ibid.

6. *Open Your Bible: Day 12, Apply It Responsibly,* shereadstruth.com, accessed 10/10/2014.

7. Commentary note on Hebrews 13 (THE VOICE), https://www.biblegateway.com/passage/?search =Hebrews+13&version=VOICE, accessed 10/02/2016.

#JesusIsWorthIt Challenge

Think about telling your own story of how you believe "Jesus Is Worth It." In light of the work God has done and is doing in our lives, we simply can't keep quiet! Besides, why wouldn't we want to share it with others?

Remember, by retelling our stories we can connect deeply with others in Christ, and those connections bring joy to us as we share and to those who hear. If you do share your story online, be sure to use the #JesusIsWorthIt hashtag so we can all find each other! I'd love to hear about it too. Please email me at stacey@staceythacker.com and tell me how God is growing your faith.

Let's draw near, let's hold fast, let's love one another, and let's keep running. He is worth it.

About the Author

Stacey Thacker is a wife and the mother of four vibrant girls. Creator of the popular blog *Mothers of Daughters*, she is a writer and speaker who loves God's Word. Her passion is to connect with women and encourage them in their walks with God. You can find her blogging at staceythacker.com and hanging out on Instagram @staceythacker and Twitter @staceythacker.

To learn more about Stacey Thacker
or to read sample chapters,
visit our website:
www.harvesthousepublishers.com

HARVEST HOUSE PUBLISHERS
EUGENE, OREGON

Fresh Out of Amazing

What do you do when everyone expects you to be amazing...and you've got nothing left to give? It's an issue all busy women share—that pressure to always be a go-getter when sometimes all you want to do is get going (and stay gone for a long time).

Try savoring some grace today. Join author and speaker Stacey Thacker as she walks you through God's mercies and shows you how to...

- identify what's dragging you down so you can find the specific encouragement you need

- increase your trust in Jesus by learning practical ways to rest when you're depleted

- accept the invitation to see God big when you're fresh out of amazing

Whether you're short on time, energy, motivation, hope, or all of the above, only one thing can bring your weary spirit back to life: Jesus.

Hope for the Weary Mom

Are you tired, overwhelmed, or feeling that you have nothing left to give? In *Hope for the Weary Mom*, bloggers Stacey Thacker and Brooke McGlothlin (creators of the online communities *Mothers of Daughters* and *The MOB Society*) lead you to the God who meets you in your mess and show you that you don't walk through life alone. You will...

- invite God into your mess
- reconnect with his heart for you
- experience the peace and freedom of walking with him

It's easy to forget that God knows you by name when you're numb with the daily grind. Join Stacey and Brooke and begin the journey from weariness to hope.